roodles

ROSE ADDERS

THIS IS A CARLTON BOOK

This edition published in 2009 by
Carlton Books Limited
20 Mortimer Street
London W1T 3JW

ISBN 978-1-84732-501-3

10 9 8 7 6 5 4 3 2

Printed in Singapore

Thank you: miss boakes, luke + roland, the family, parker, lamy, normal and you.

roodles

Create your own Smutty Scribblings,
Pervy Portraits, and Deviant Drawings

From the twisted mind of Rose Adders

CARLTON

Draw in this book

Color in the images

Fill in the drawings

Stick things in it

Fill the pages with emotion

Cover the pages in liquid

Punish the pages – they've been naughty!

It's your book . . . use it!

Who's blocking YOUR sun?

What could you measure?

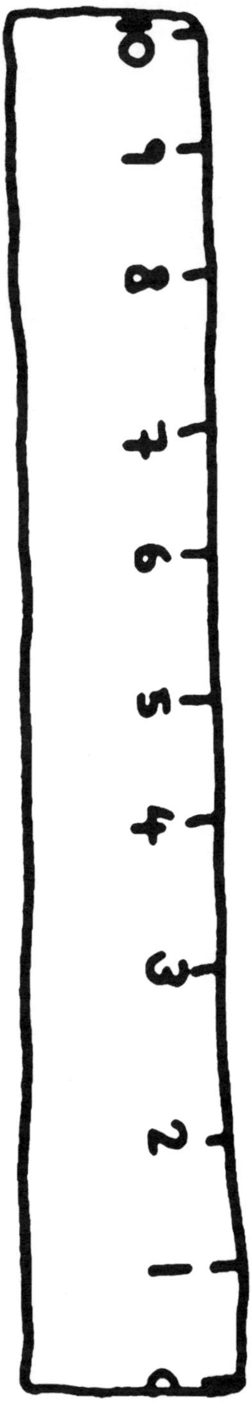

Is this something you didn't know about your parents?

What could these be?

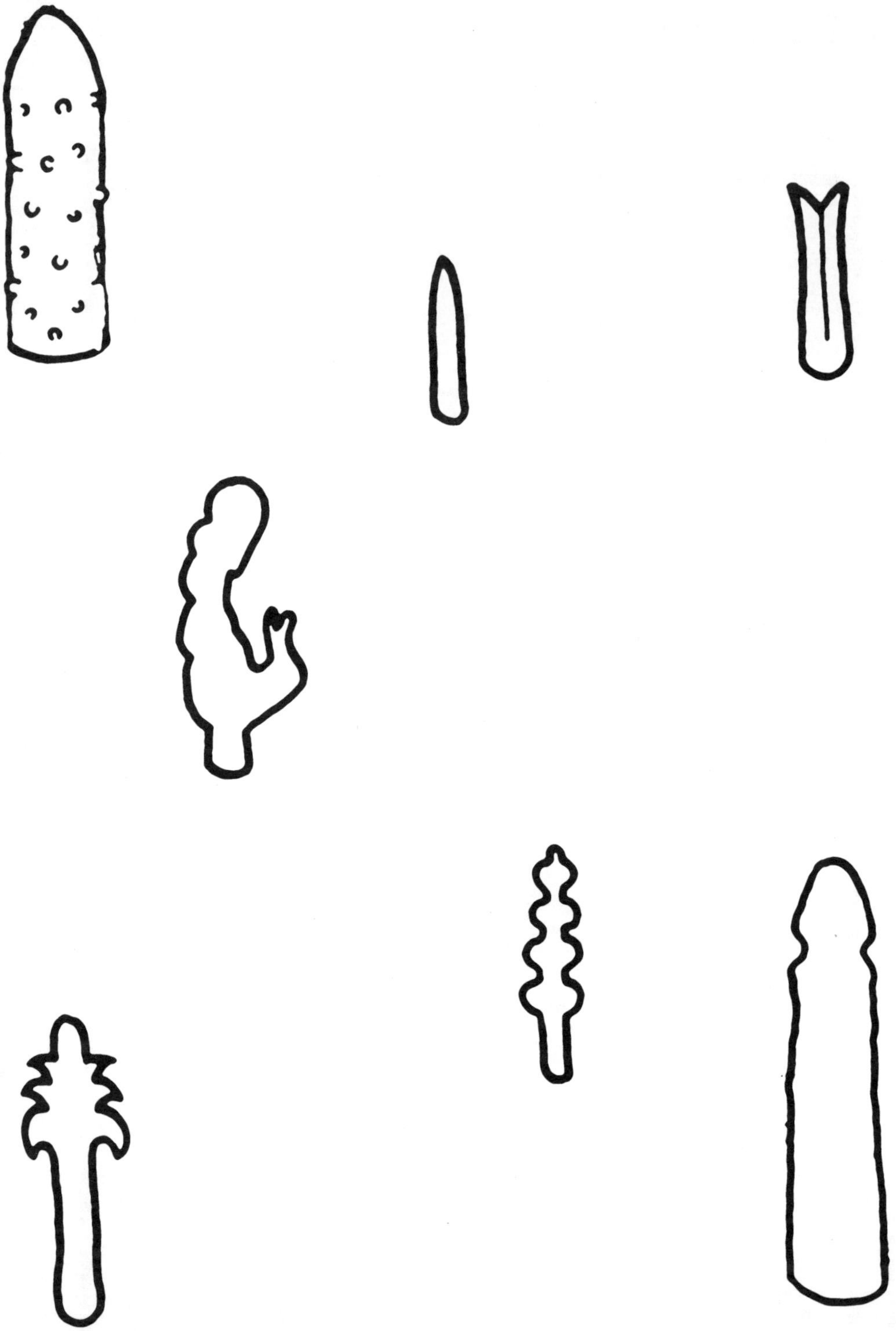

What are you spying on?

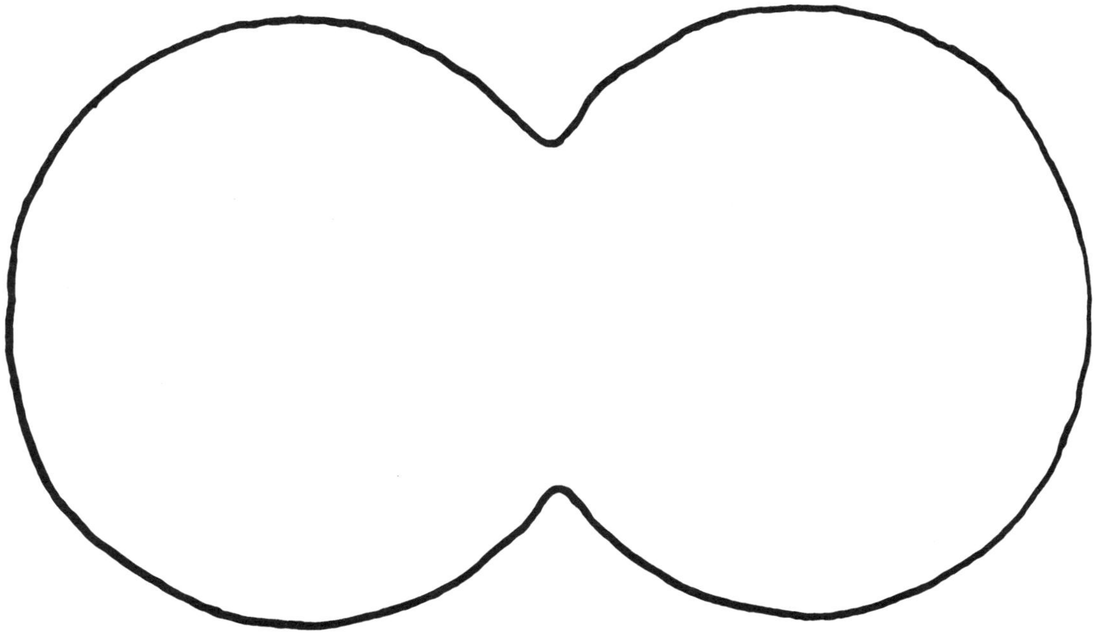

Give this guy a handful

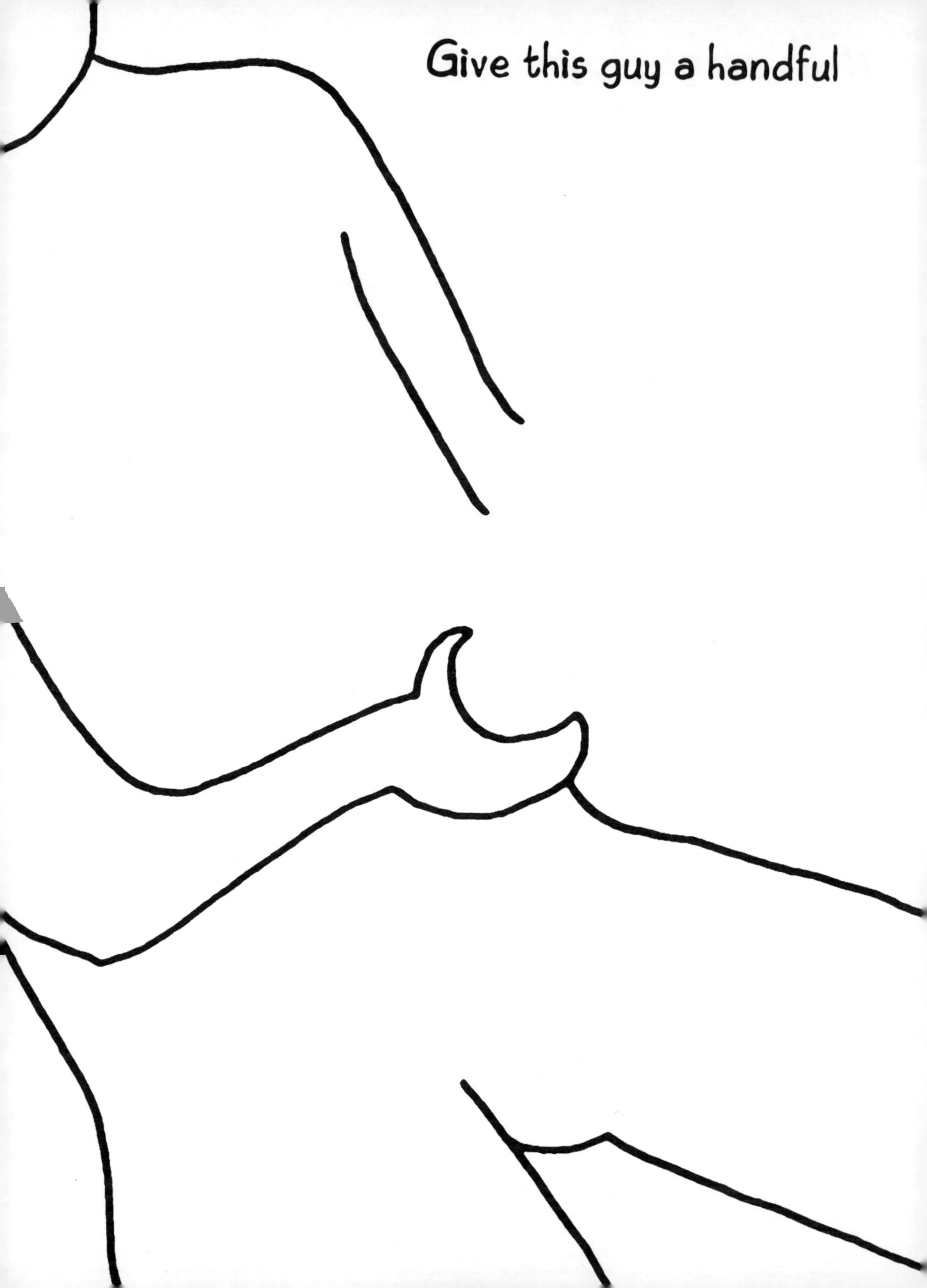

Make an animal from this

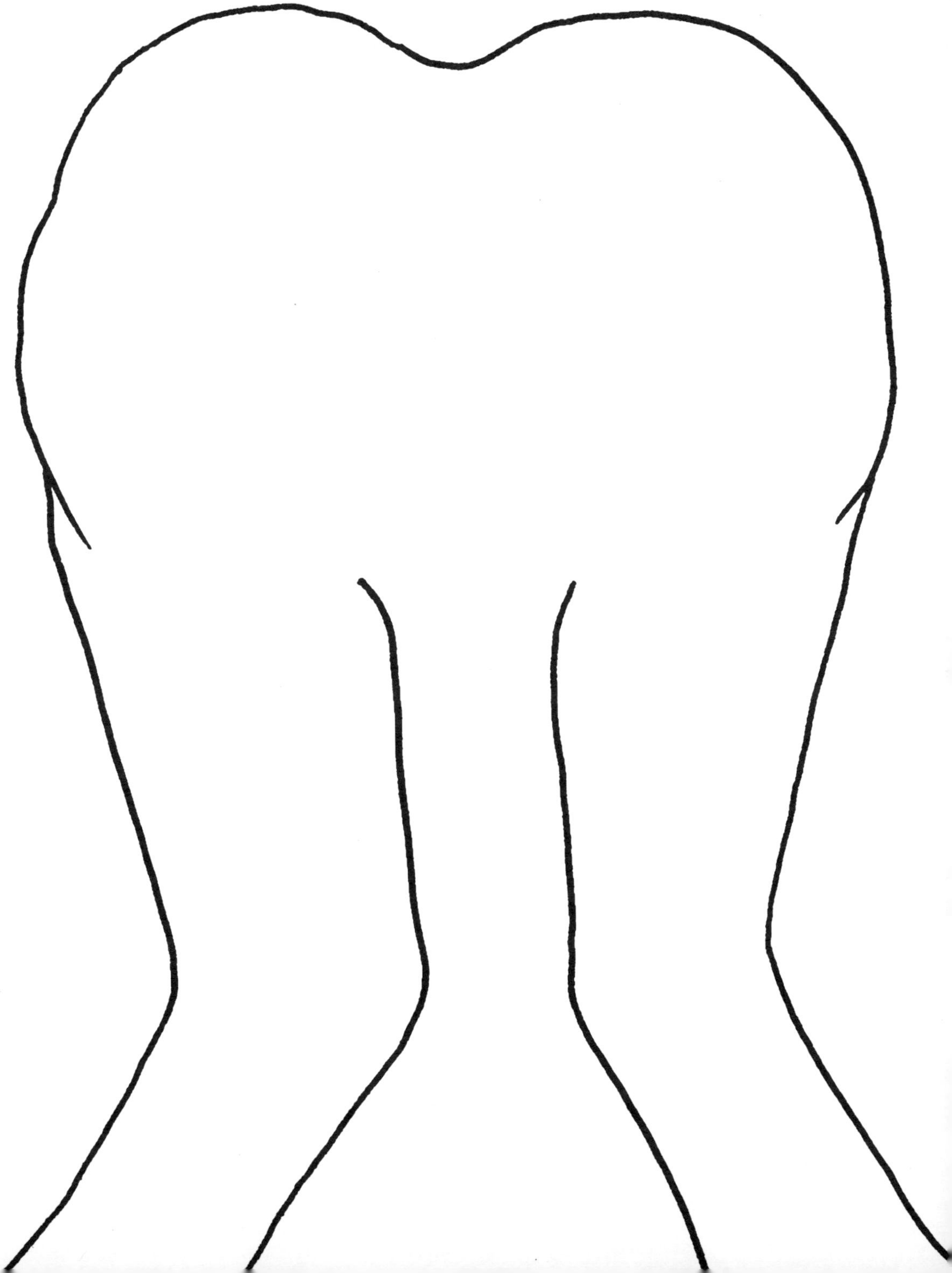

Nice shoes!

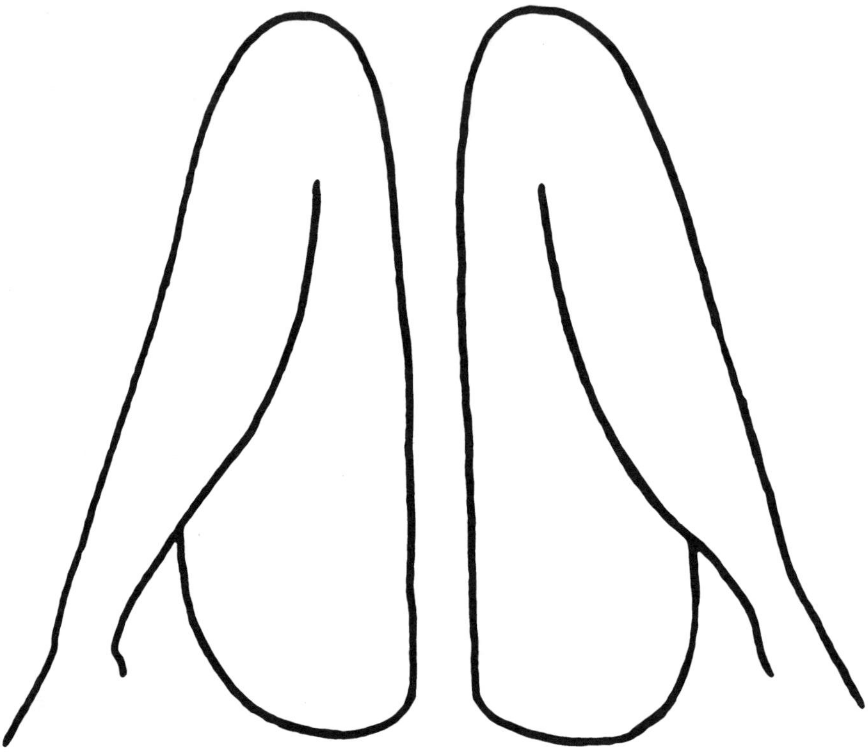

Finish the flasher

Get the cock to the crackers...

Lines and lines and lines and lines and lines...

Journey to the centre of...

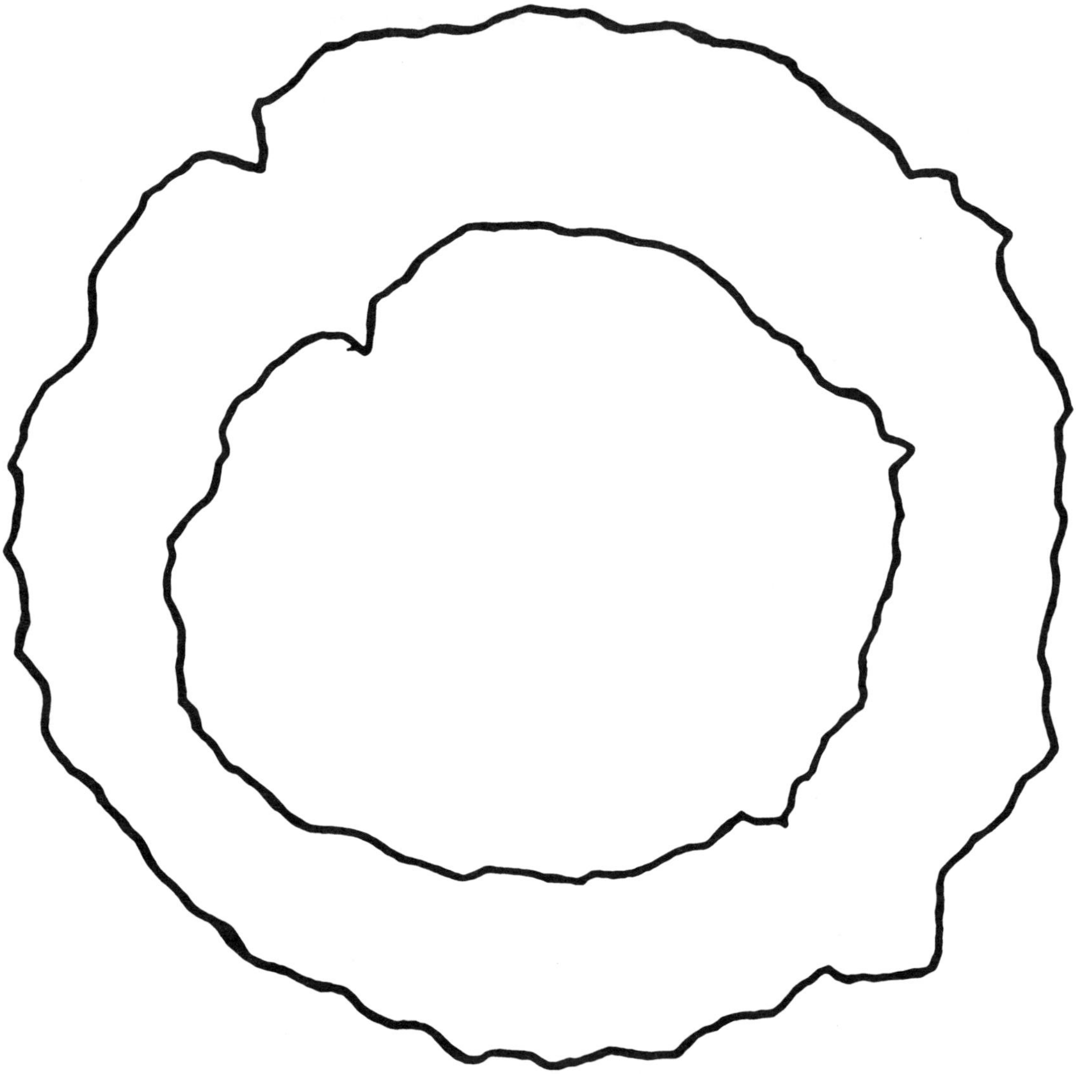

Alien eyes or funny fruit?

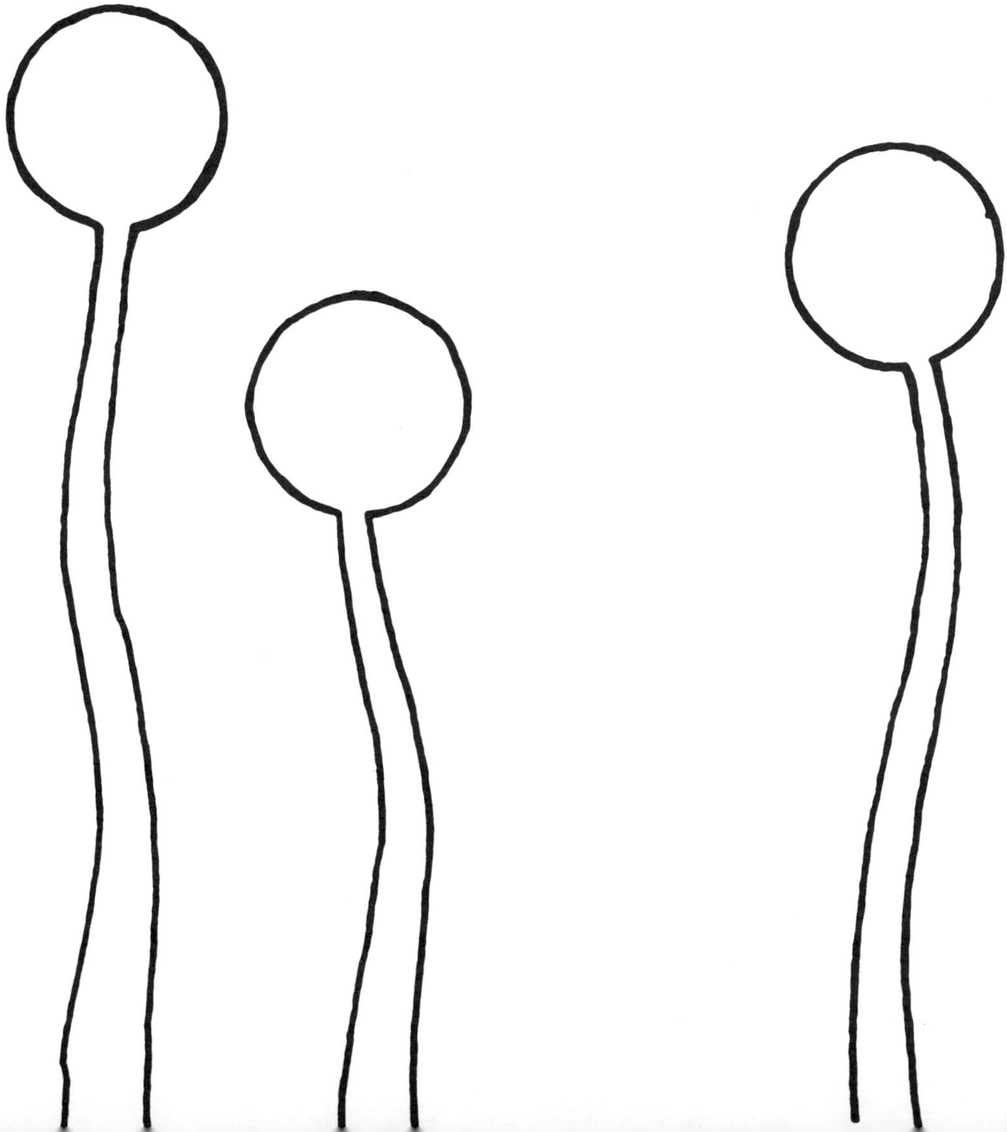

From a different dimension

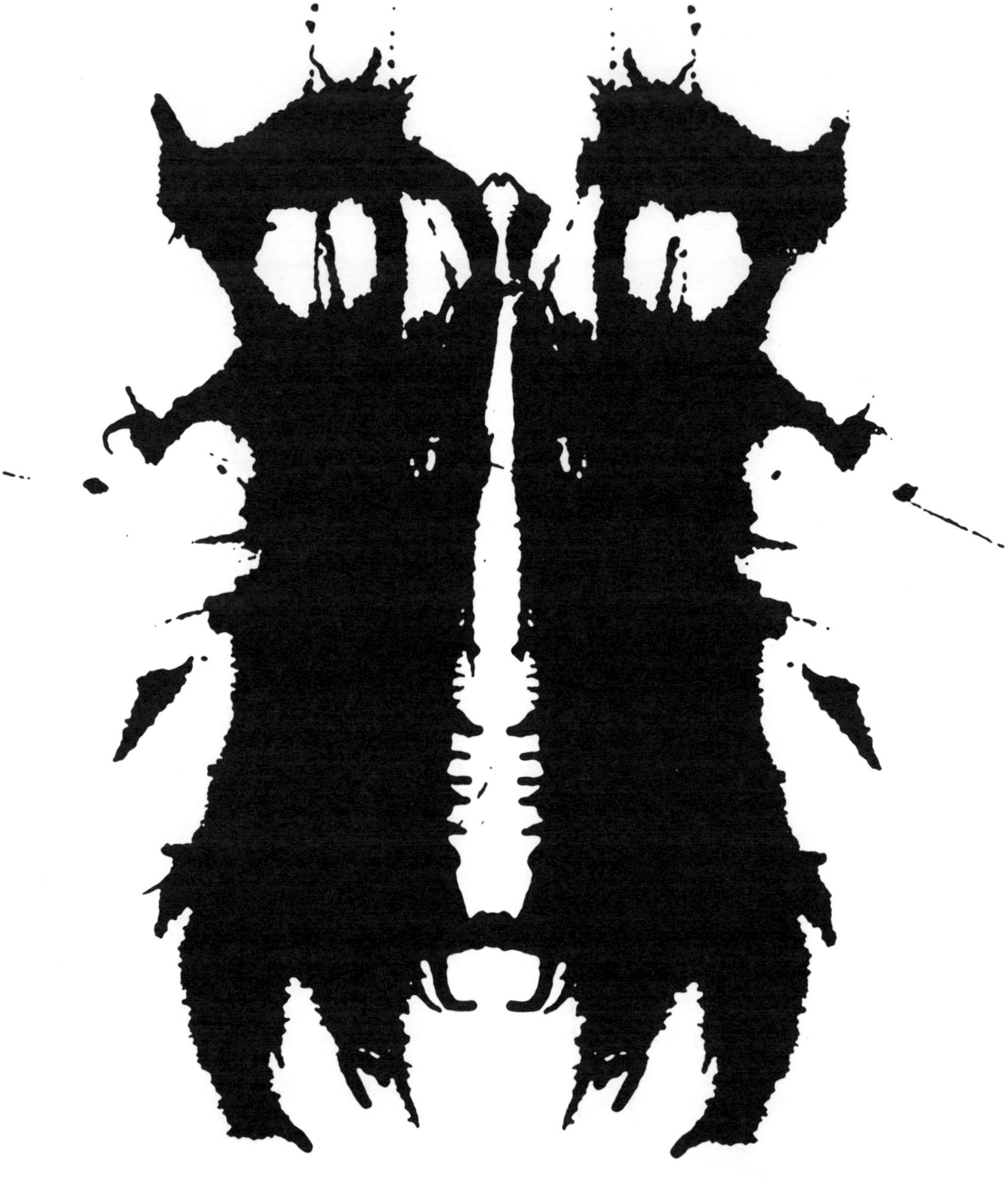

Eeeeeeeeeee splat!

What's popped out of the magic hat?

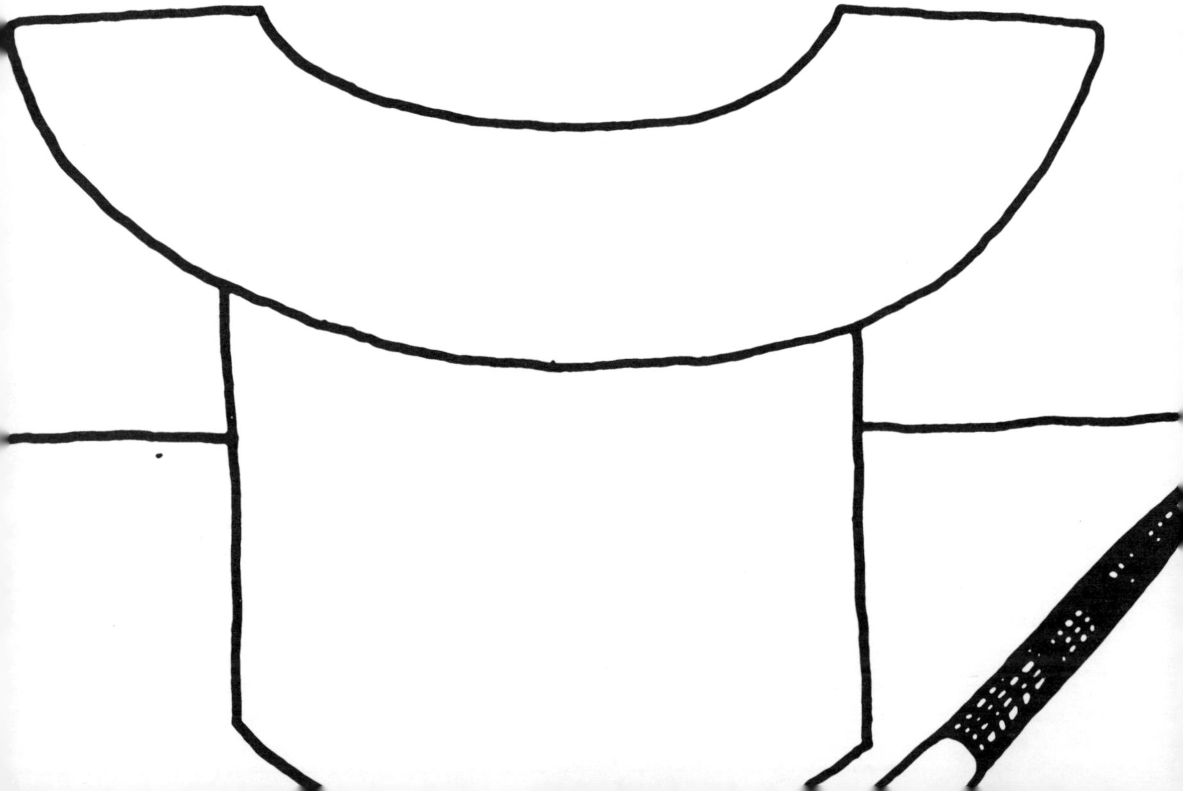

Draw your queen

Make your own jigsaw

Is that a pistol in your fist?

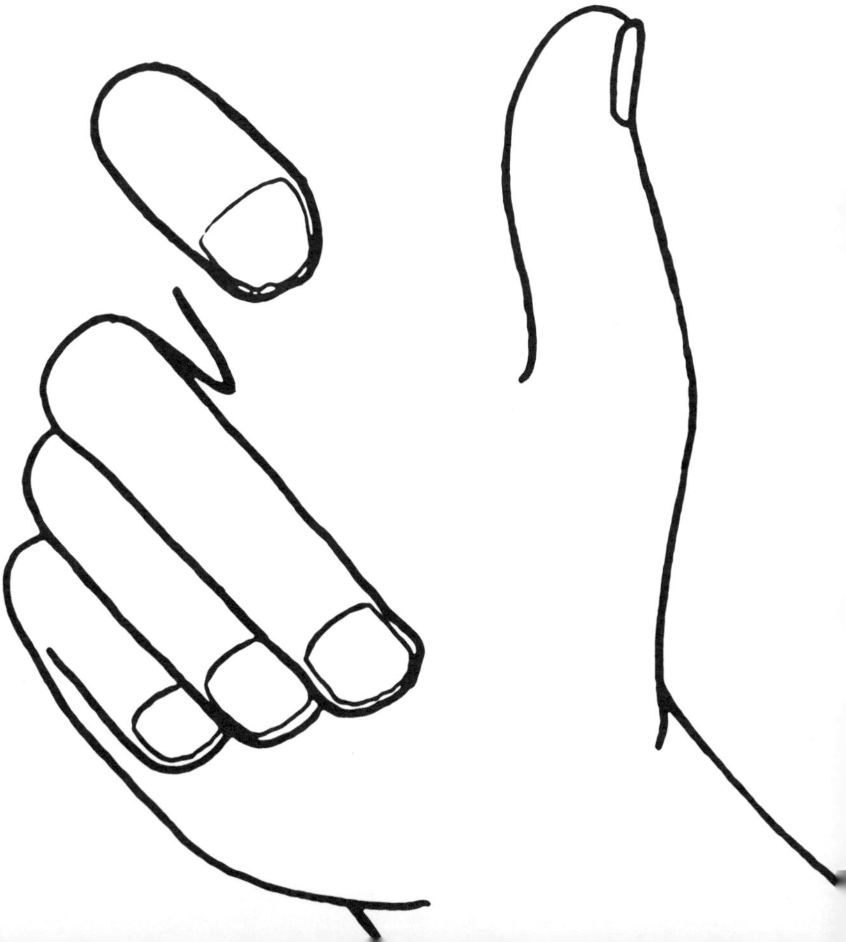

What's this wobbly roundshape?

Where was the chopper dropped?

Complete the pointy instrument

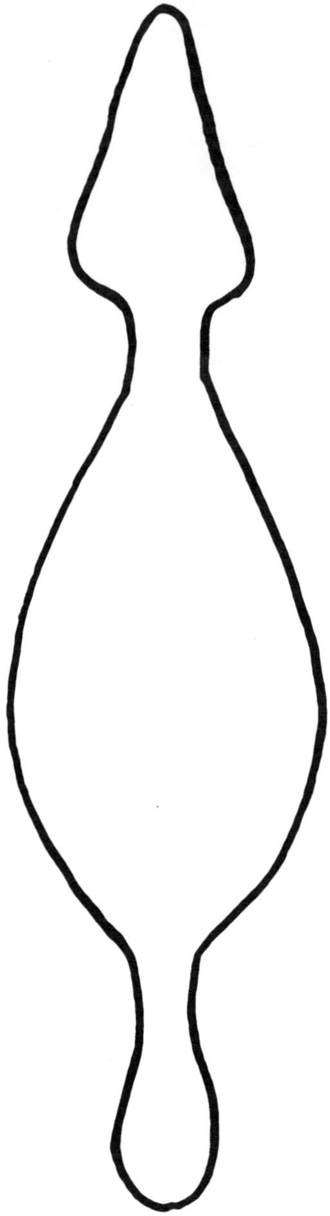

Make your own stamp

Udder dog or cat's bum?

What's going on in this bed?

What do you think is dangling overhead?

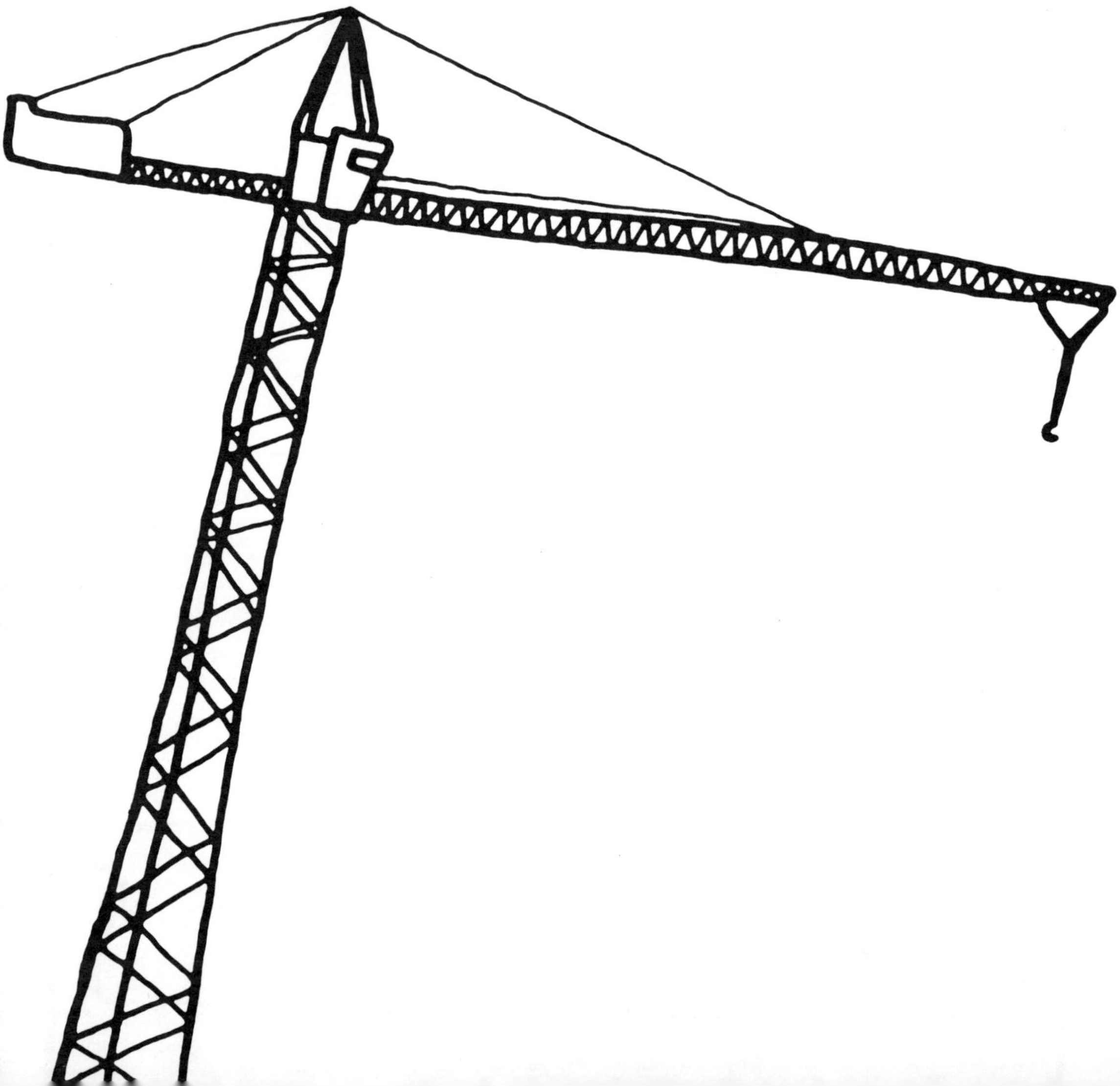

What's stuck in the fishnets?

What sort of creature is this?

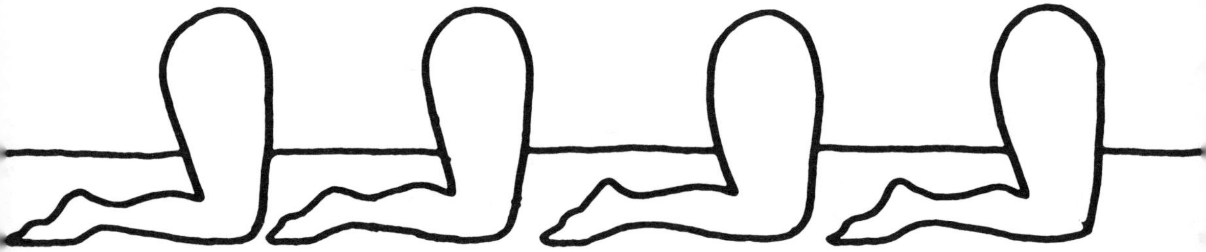

Are these faces, pills, or bulletholes?

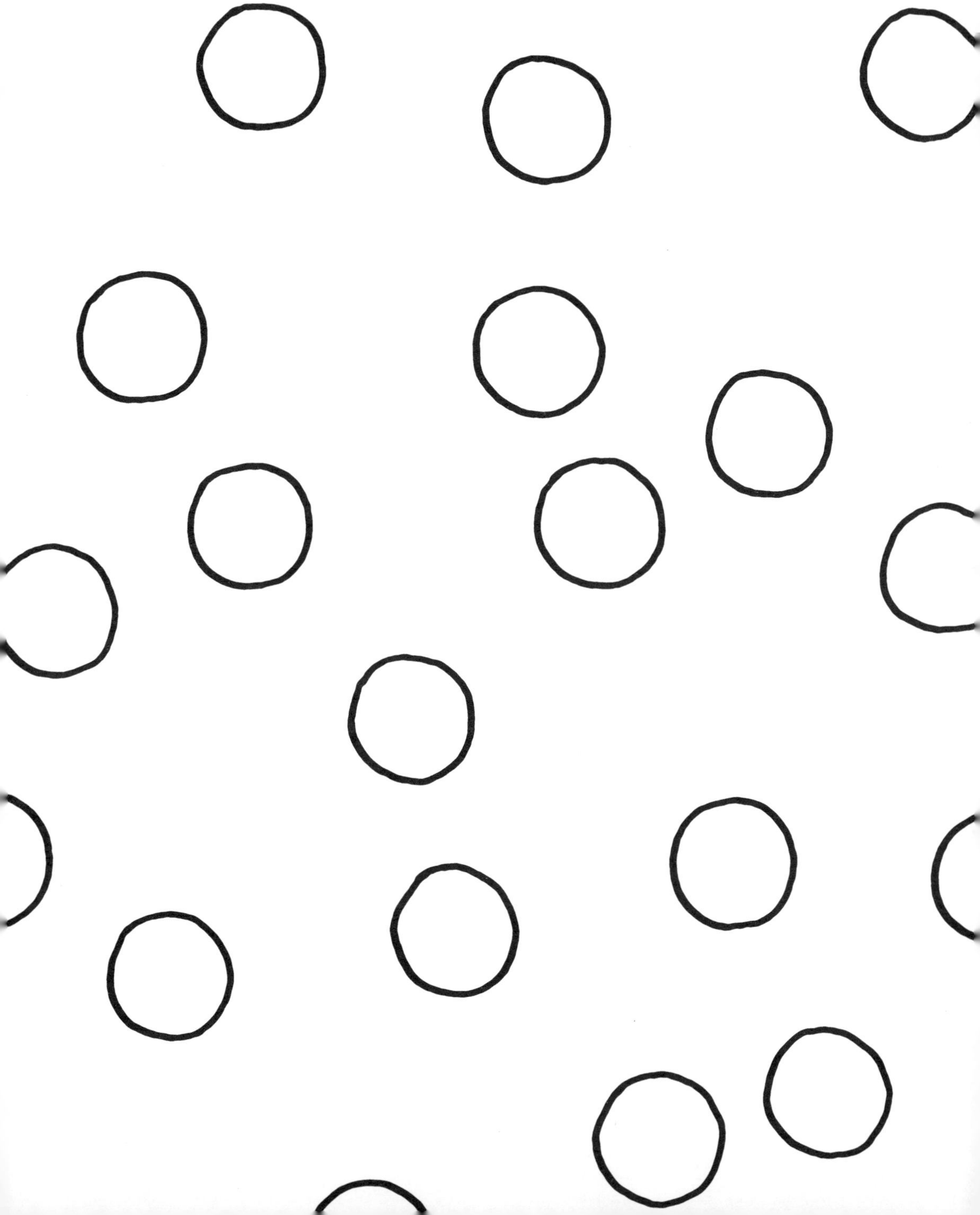

Want to go trolley-riding?

What's your sign?

Give the skeleton a bone?

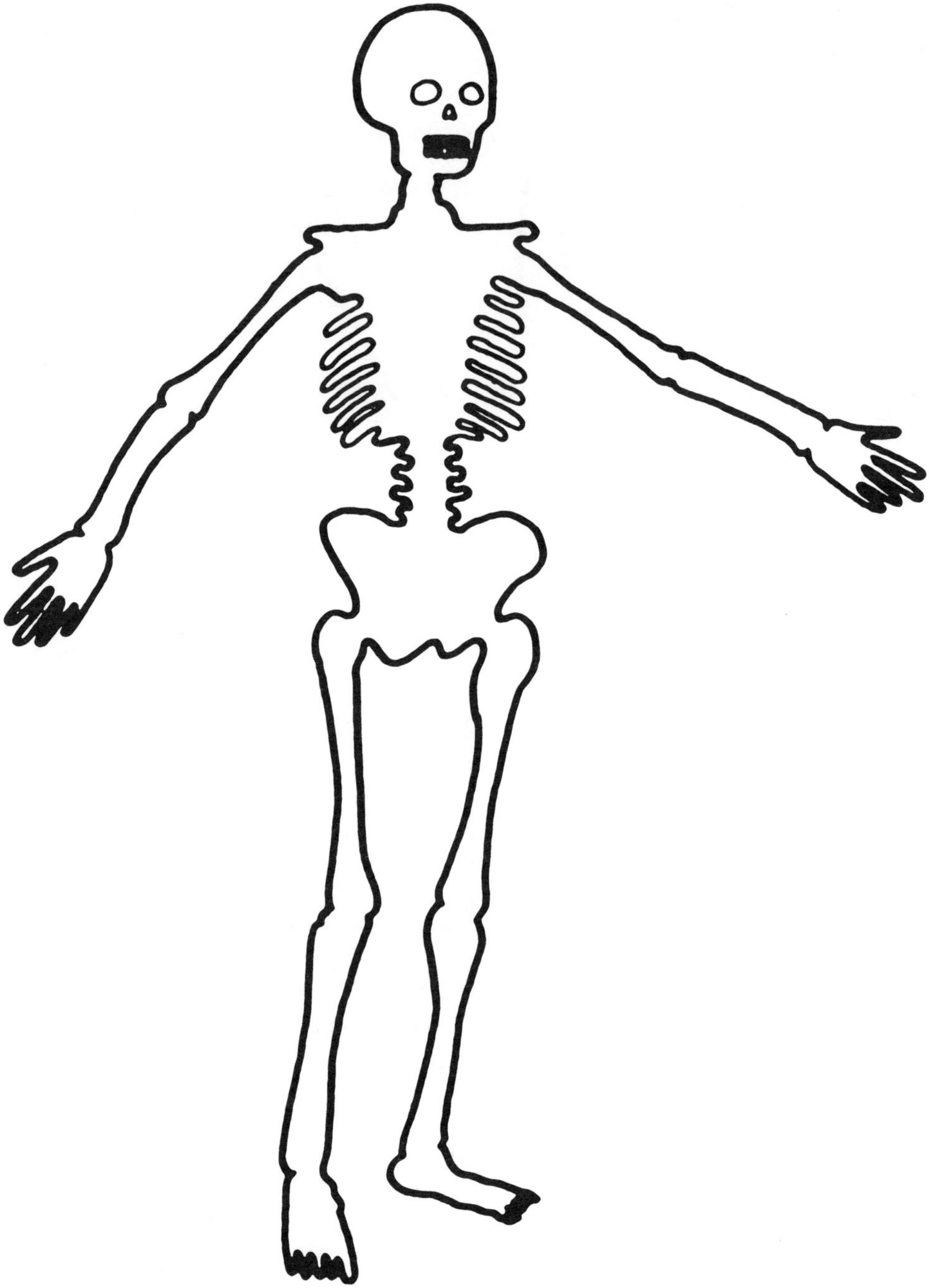

What's in the trunk?

Hanging out!

Half-man, half-?

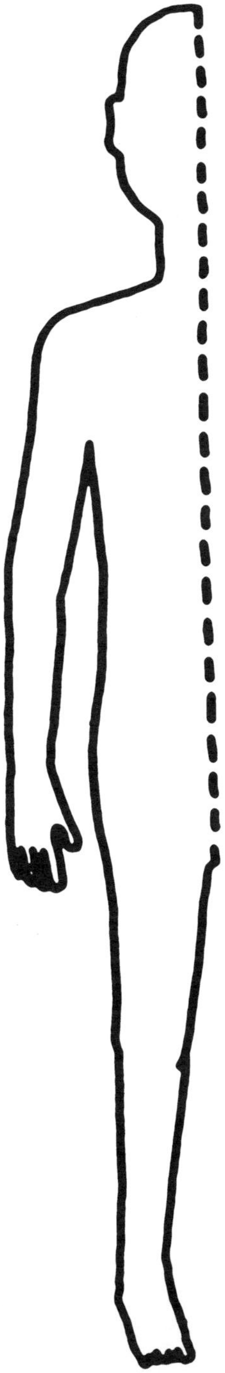

What could these be?

Twins?

Can you make something out of this?

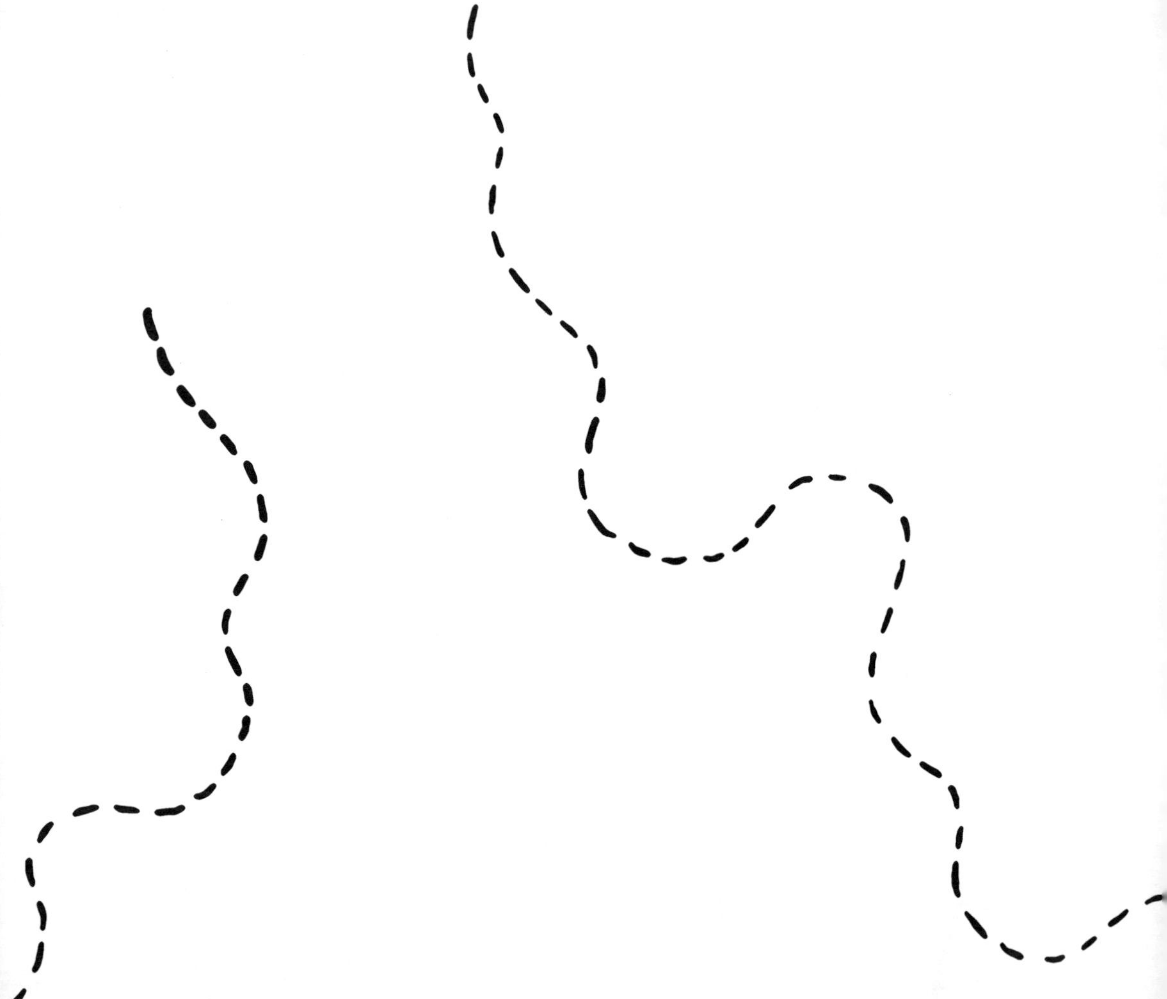

It's a wabbit!

Where does food come from?

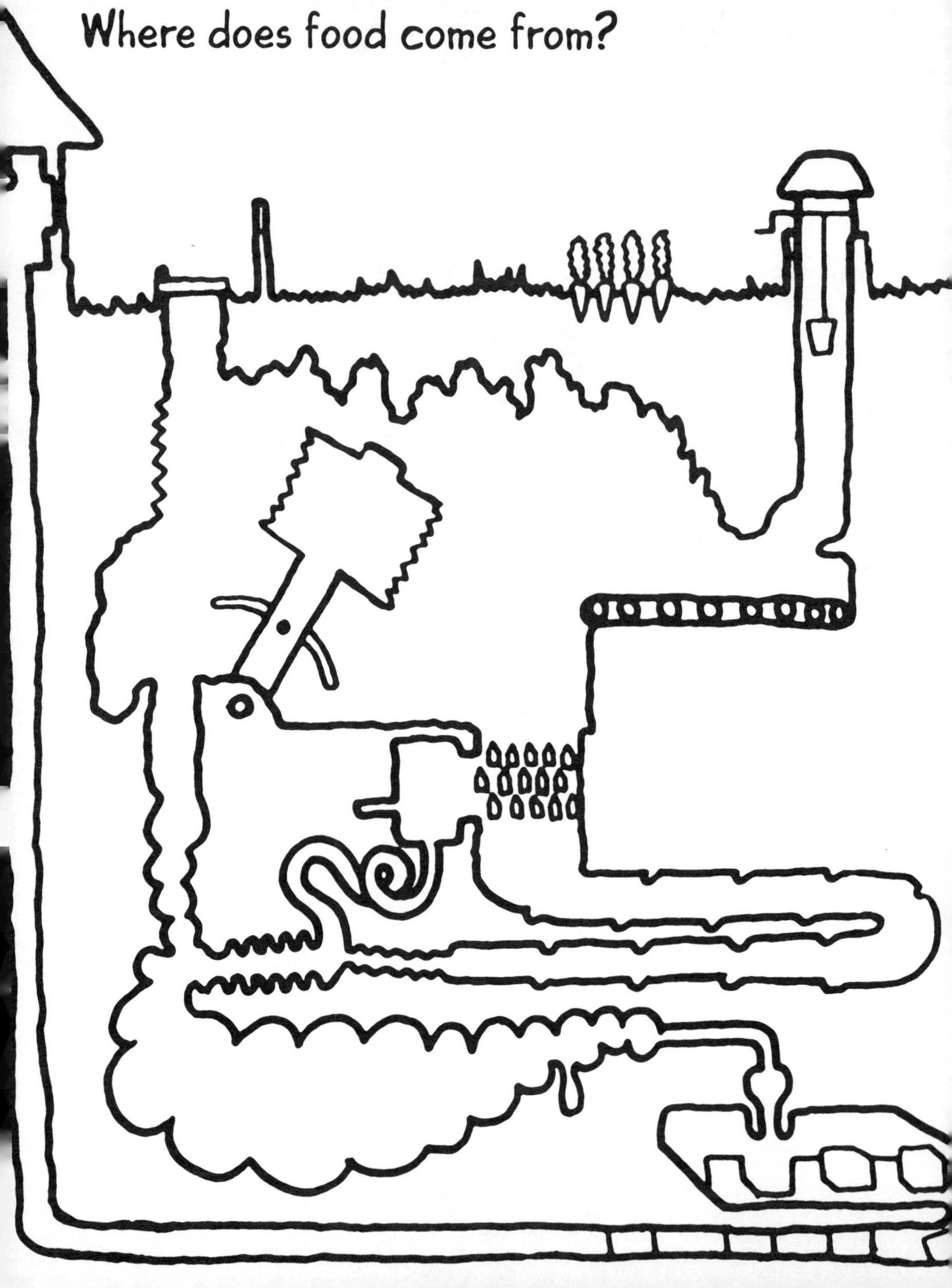

What's this little birdie saying?

What's packed like sardines?

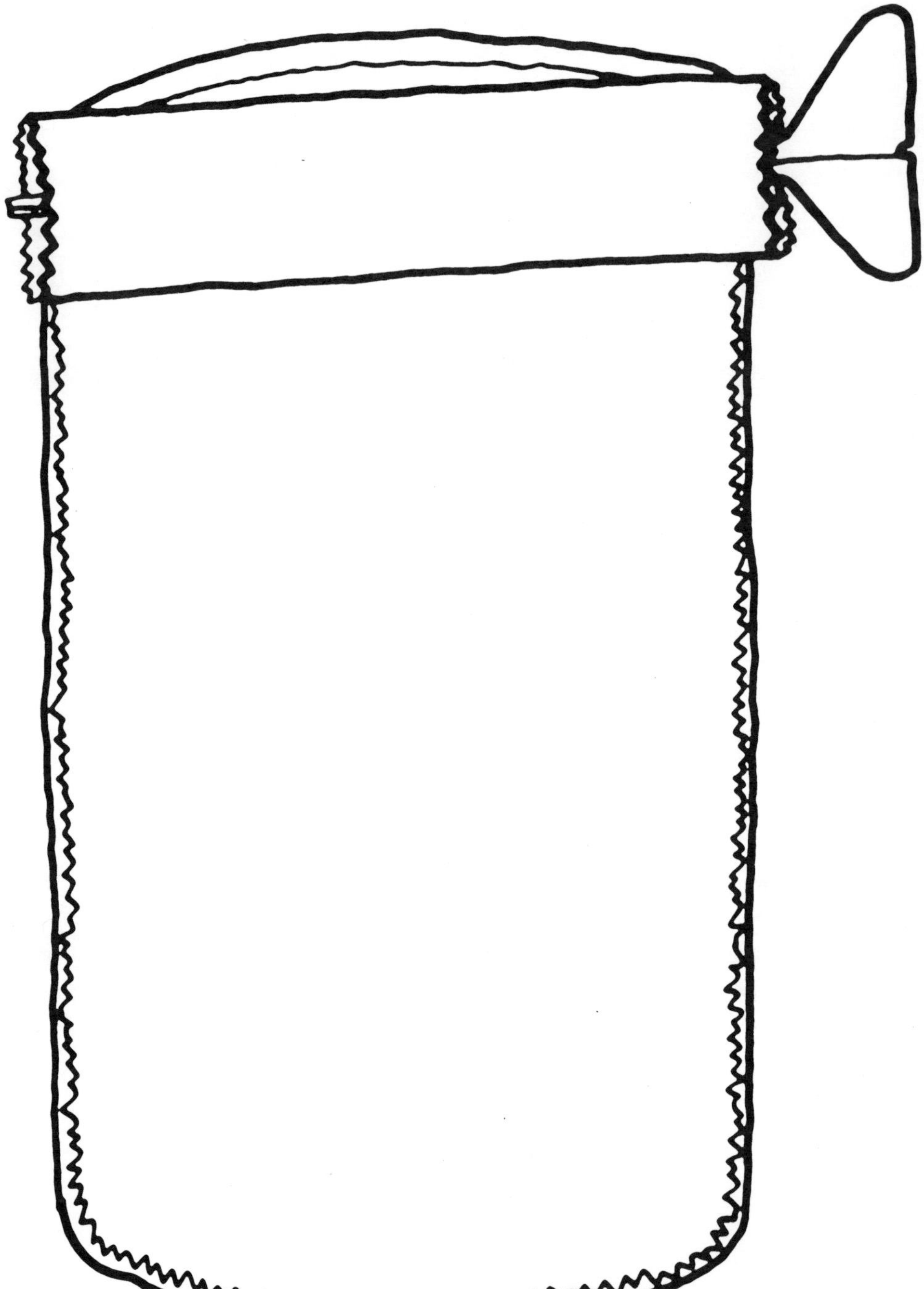

Who the hell is that?

Silhouettes...

Hey, ugly dude

Give the horse a magical horn

Draw your old school wall

Paint the pan

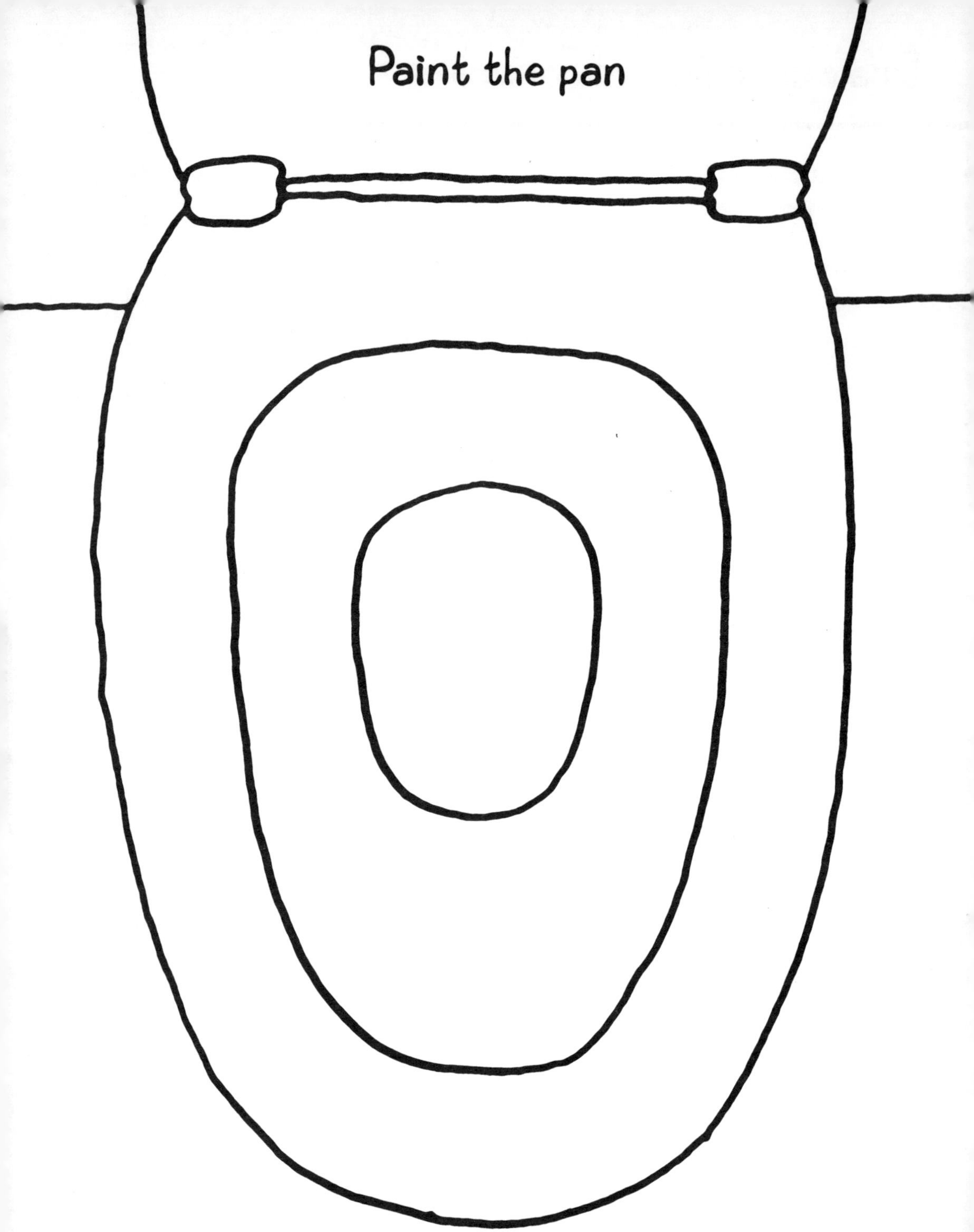

Life drawing class

What's on the operating table?

Something under the table?

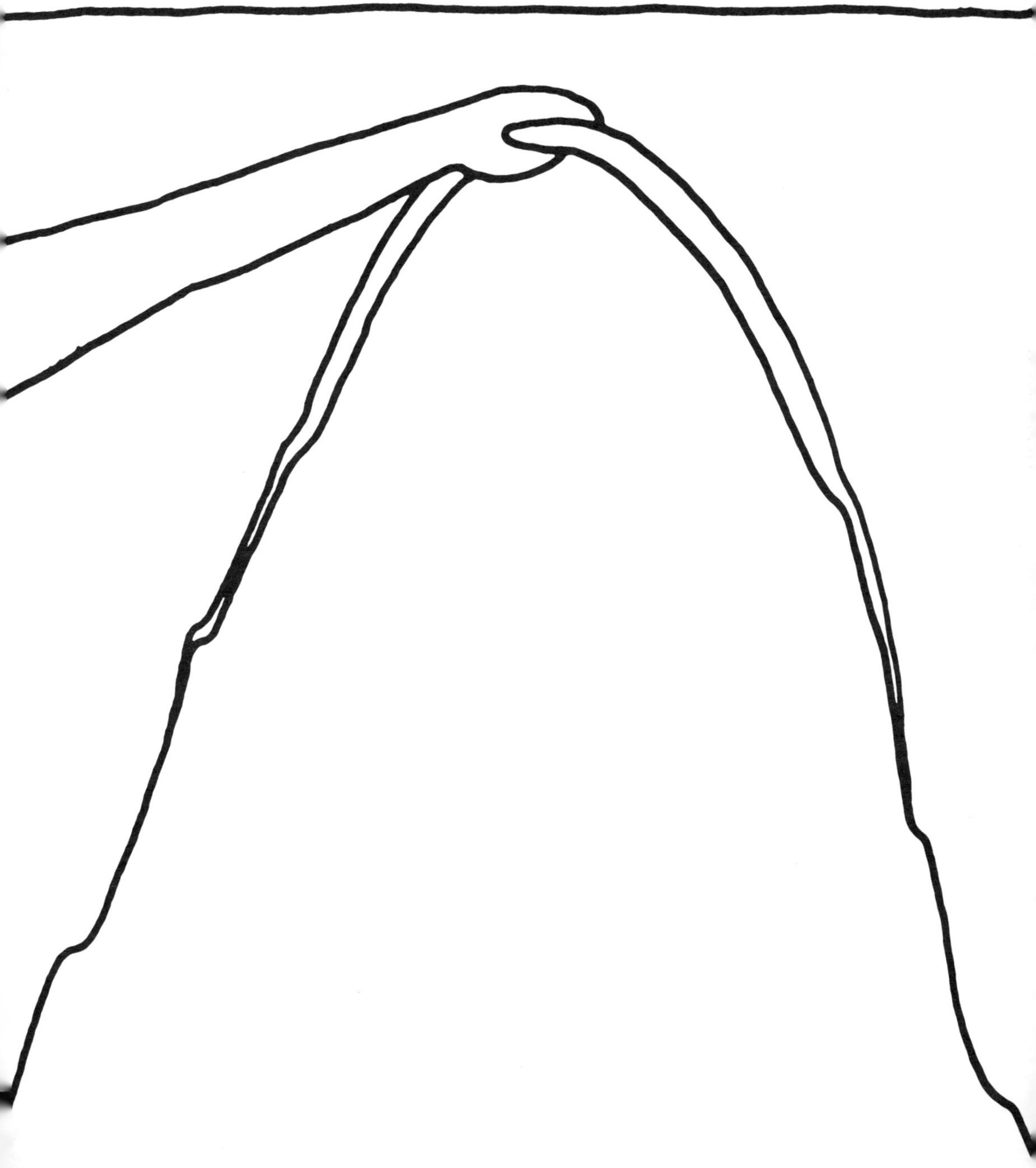

Who's chewing on the new candy bar?

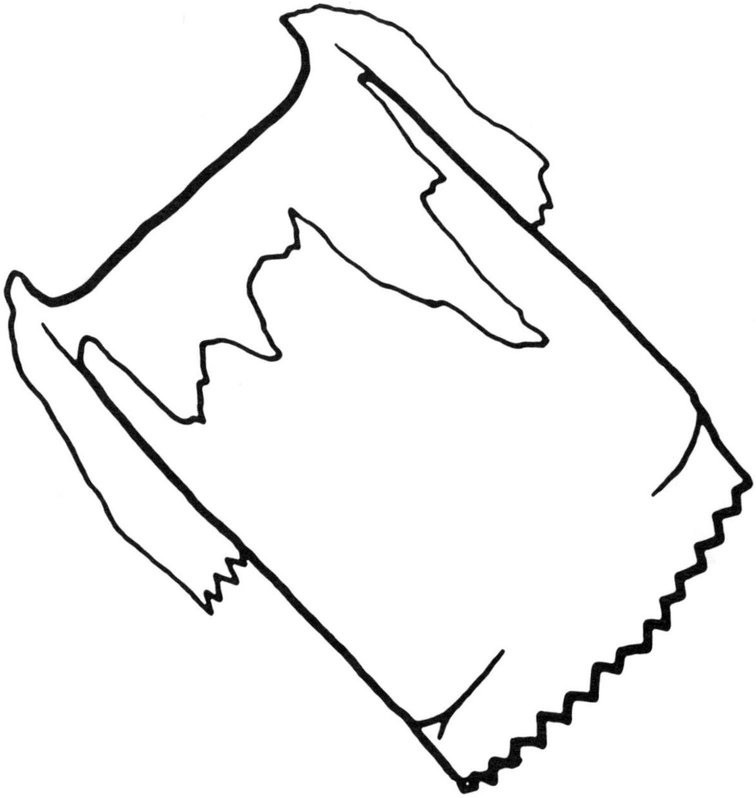

Tumblers!

Complete the toolbox

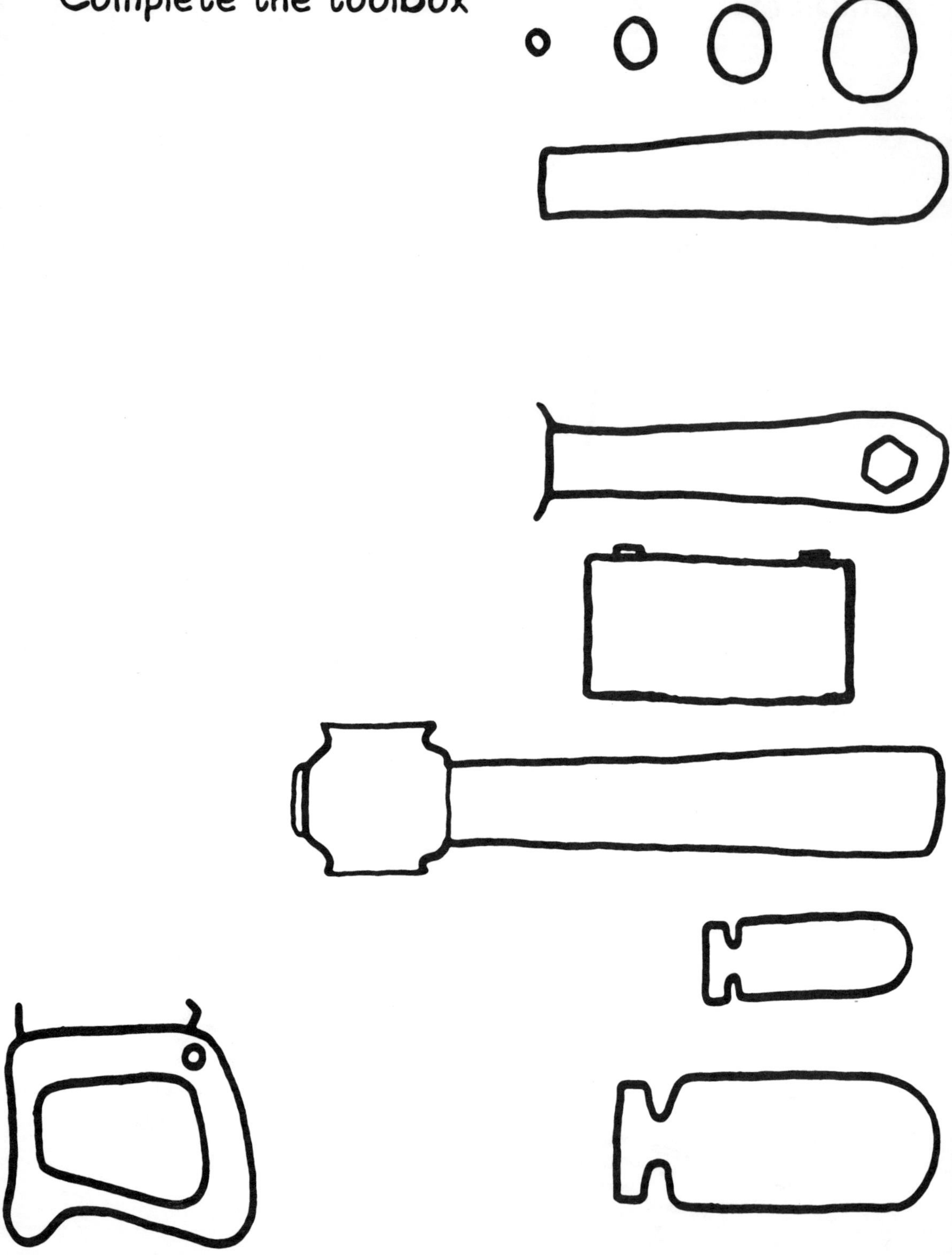

What's up Big Ben?

What else has been sucked up?

Who's the dogsbody?

You found an old polaroid

What's been left in the rock star's dressing room?

Hang out your dirty washing

Who's hanging out in the park?

Have fun on the slippery slide

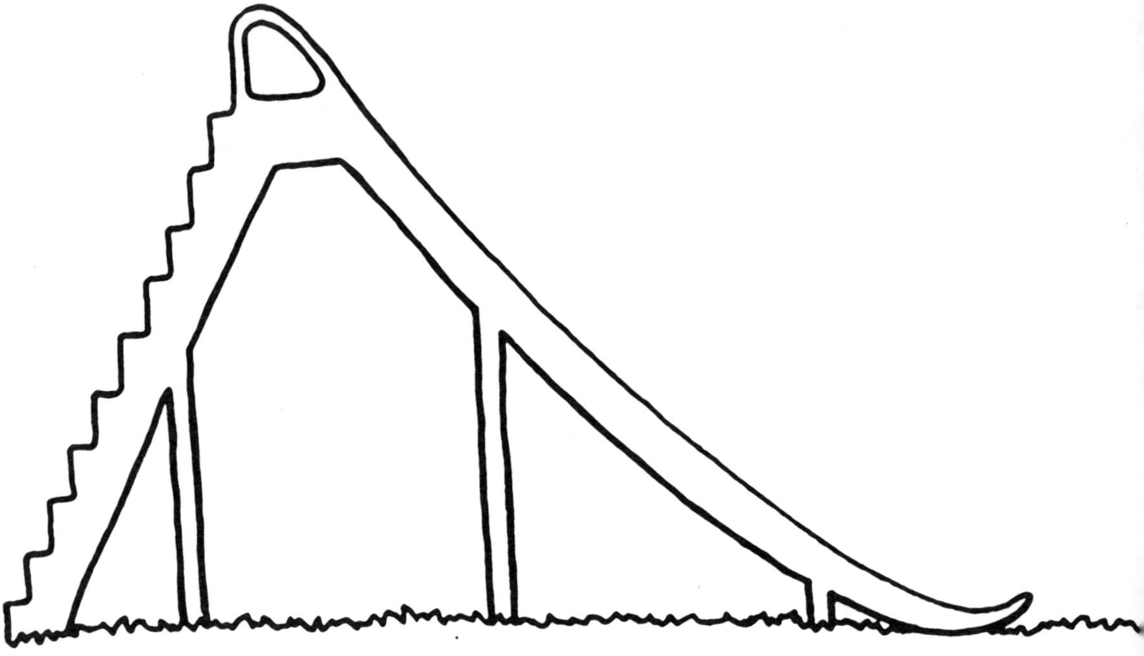

Draw the shadows

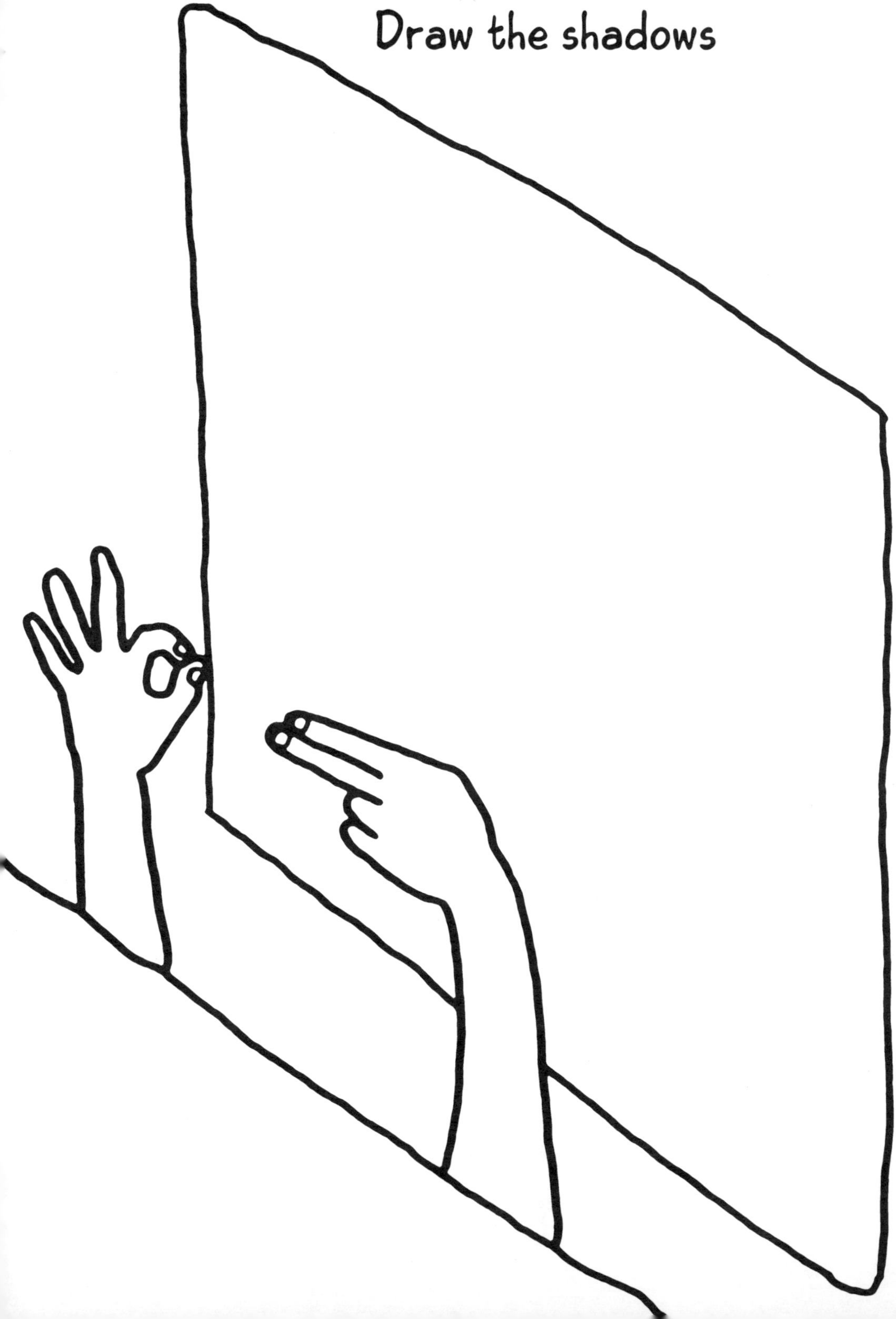

Save Dave!

Dave needs a relaxing seat

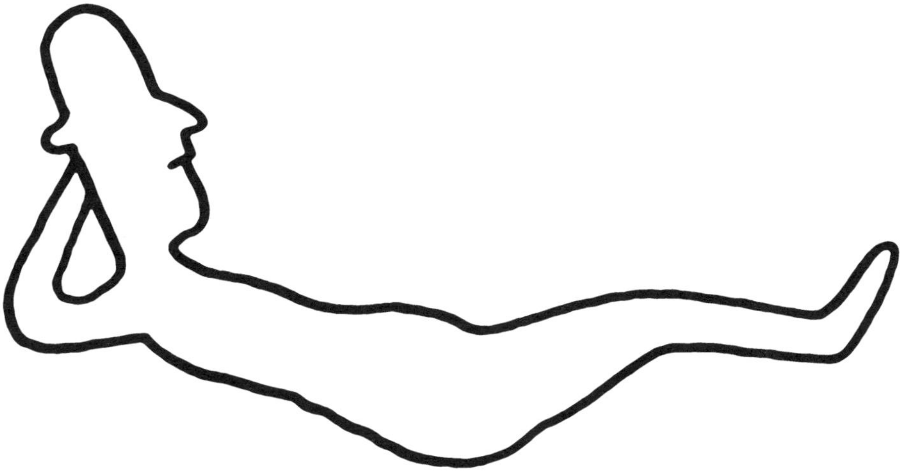

What has grown wings?

Finish off the exotic dancers

What's the frog catching?

Scary shouting old baglady!

Who's in diapers?

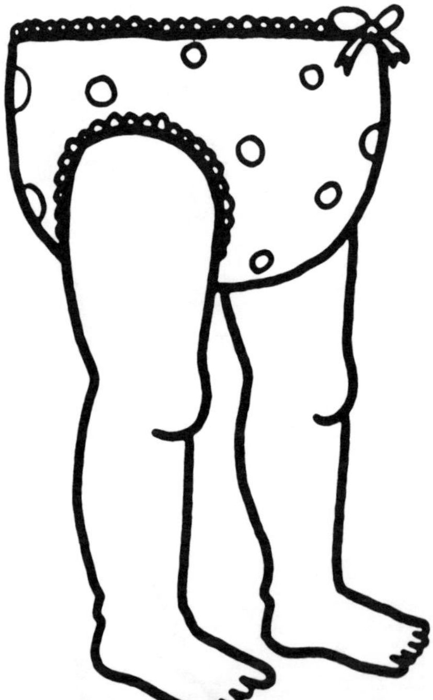

Eurgh!

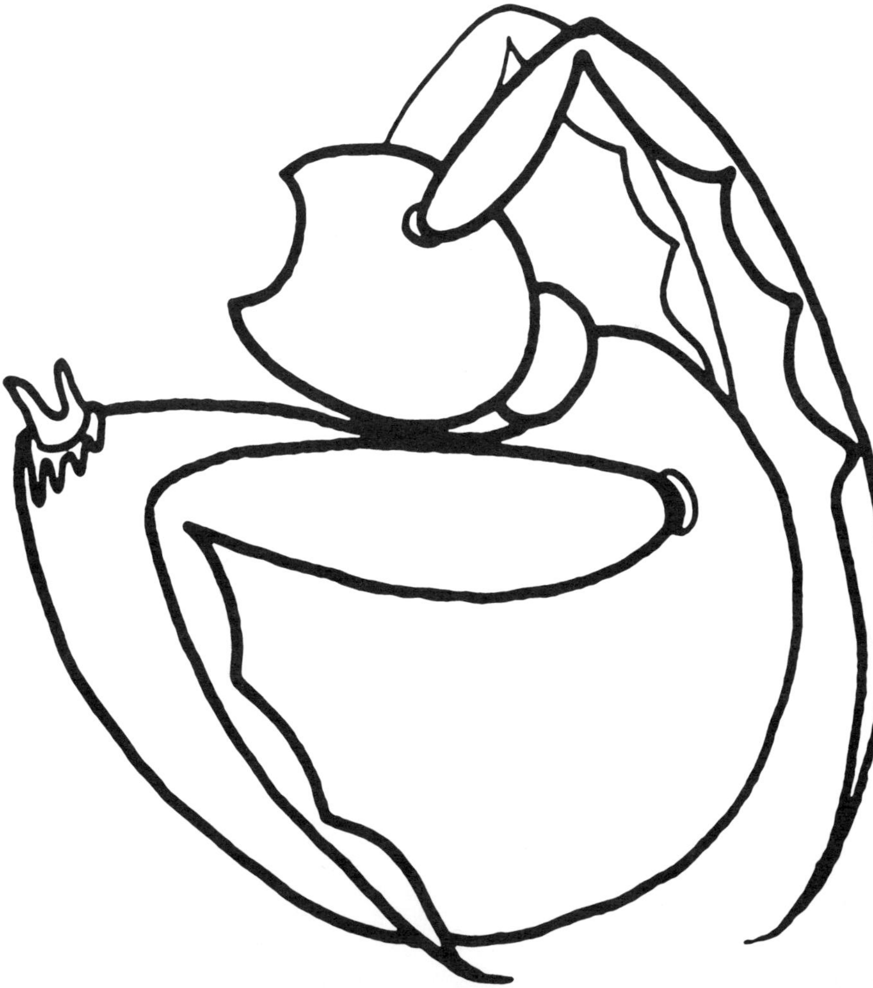

You will obey!

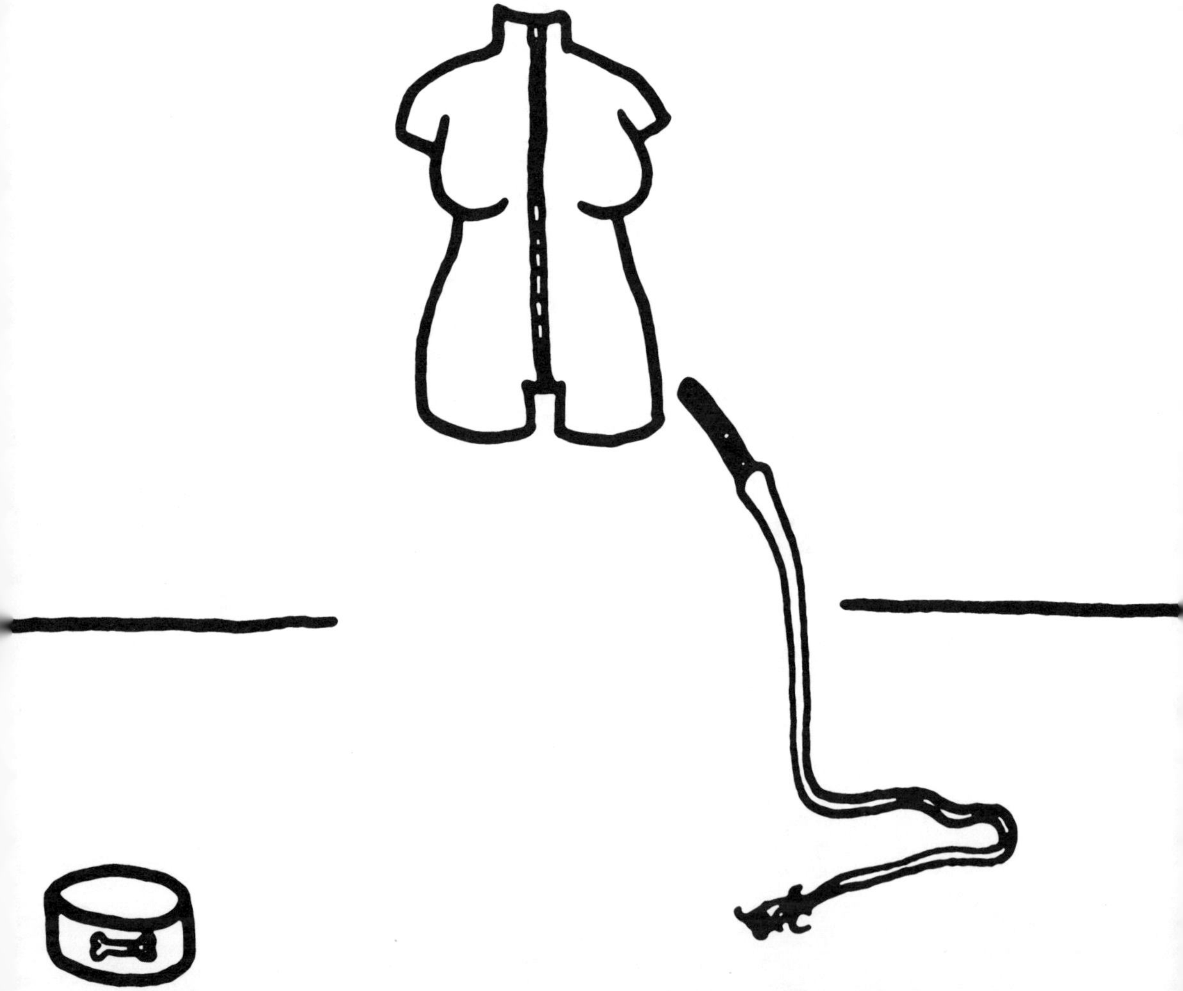

Cut something

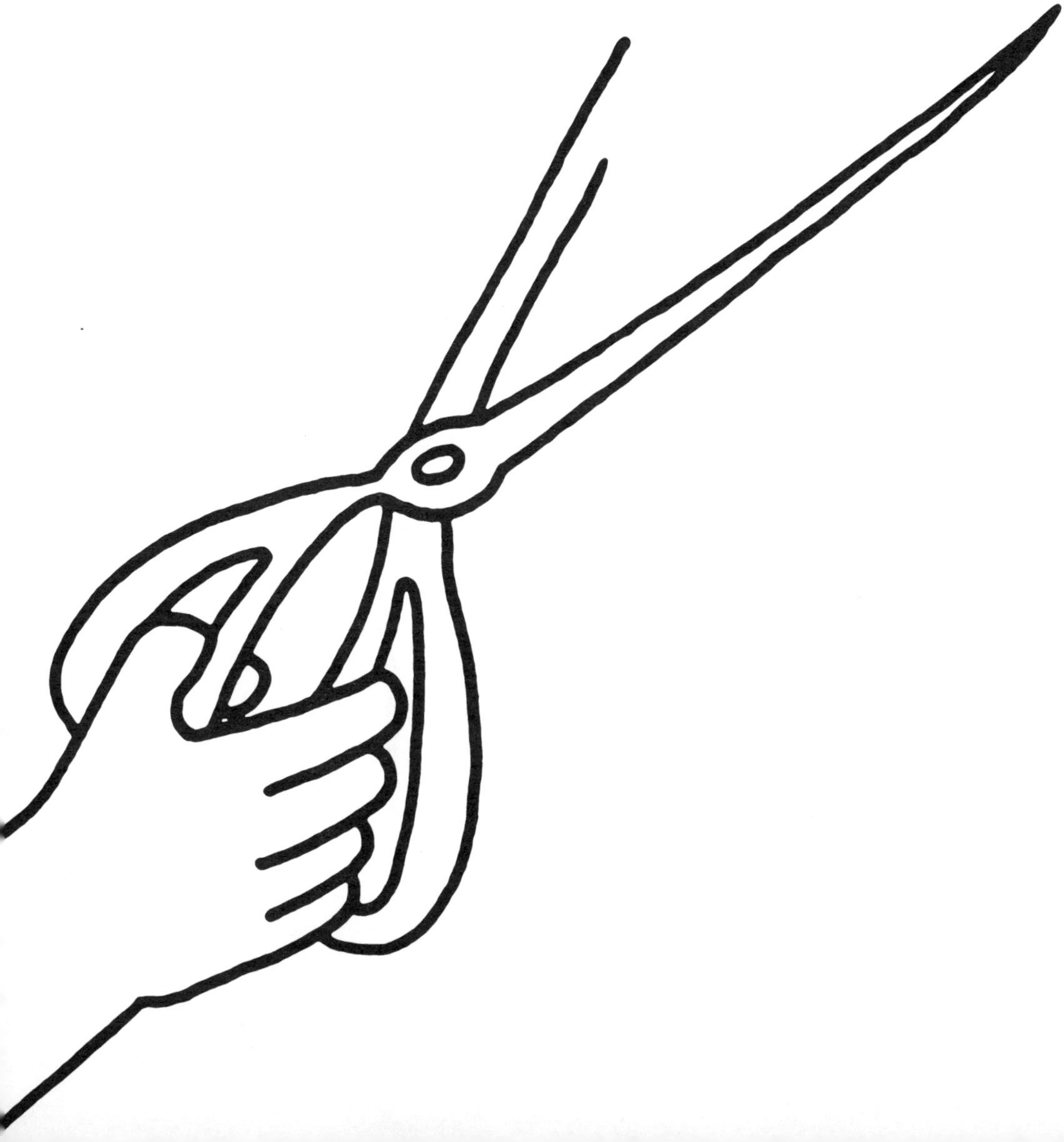

What is Dave up to?

Ug, my brain hurts

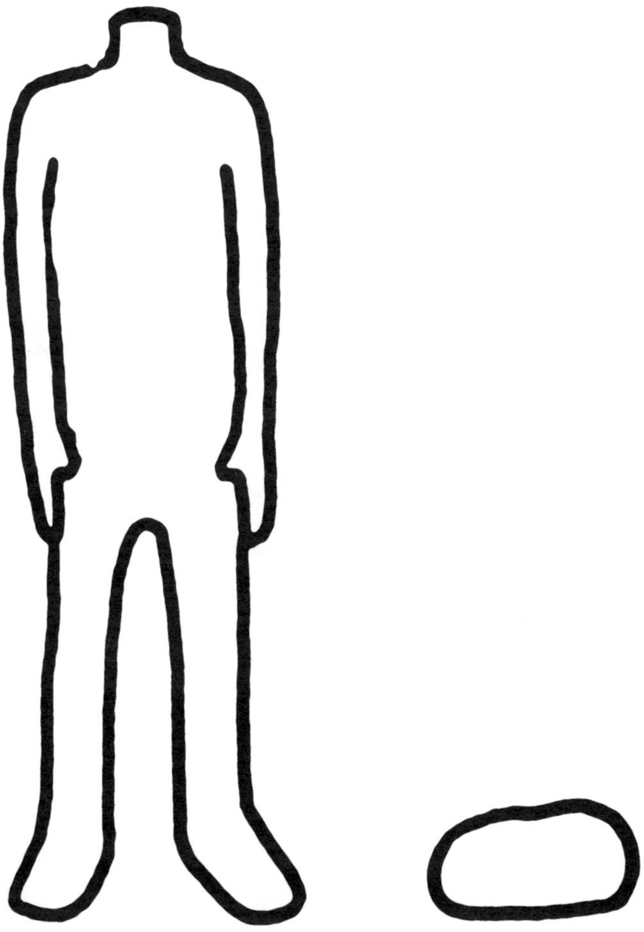

Help the large lady perform The Nutcracker

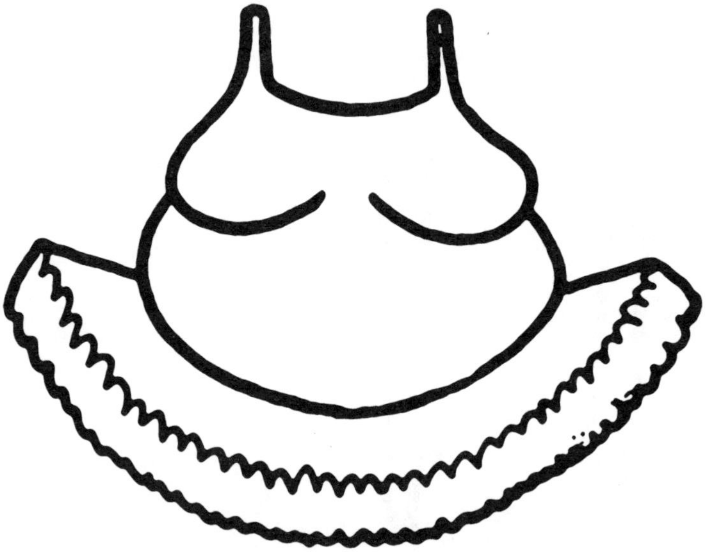

Is that a hat?

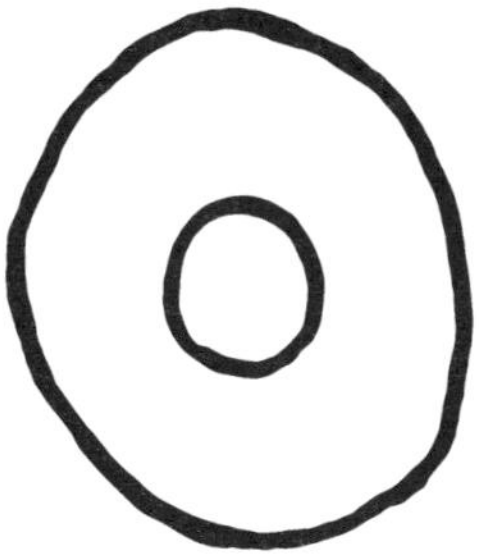

Who's in chains?

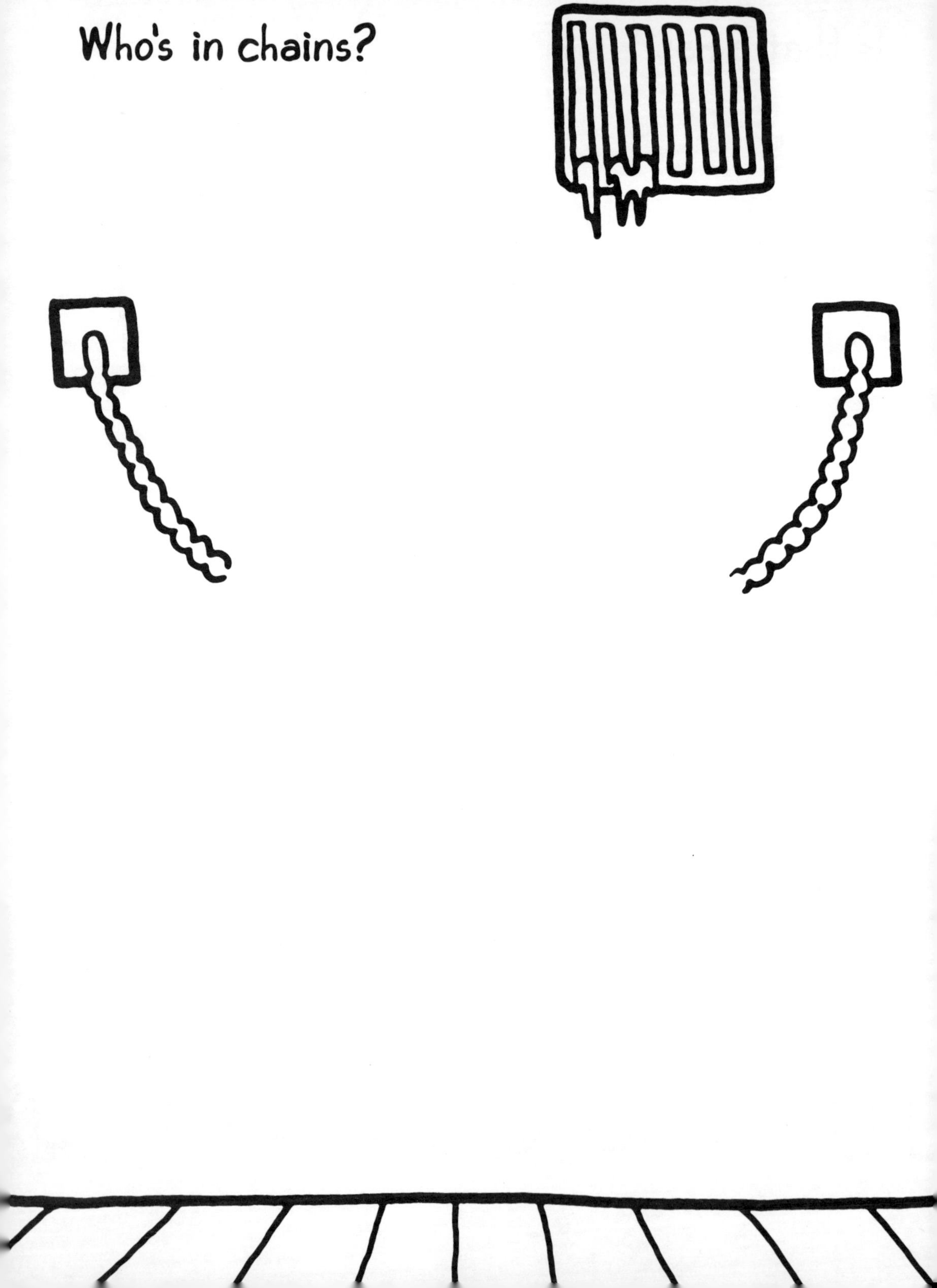

What is Dave riding?

Who's in the window?

What's happening on the back seat of the bus?

Fill the fruit bowl

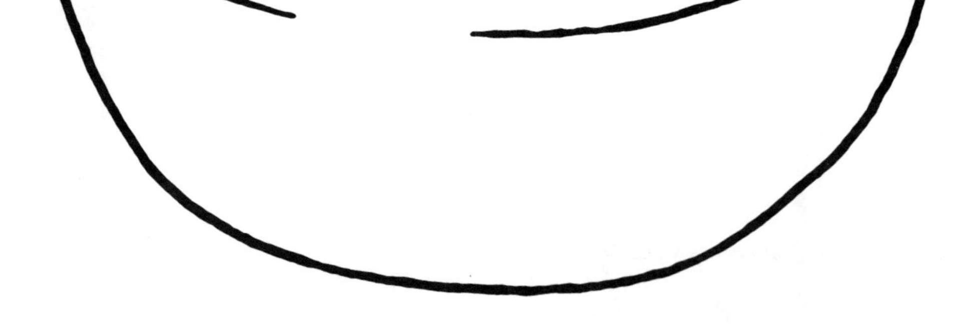

What's in the case?

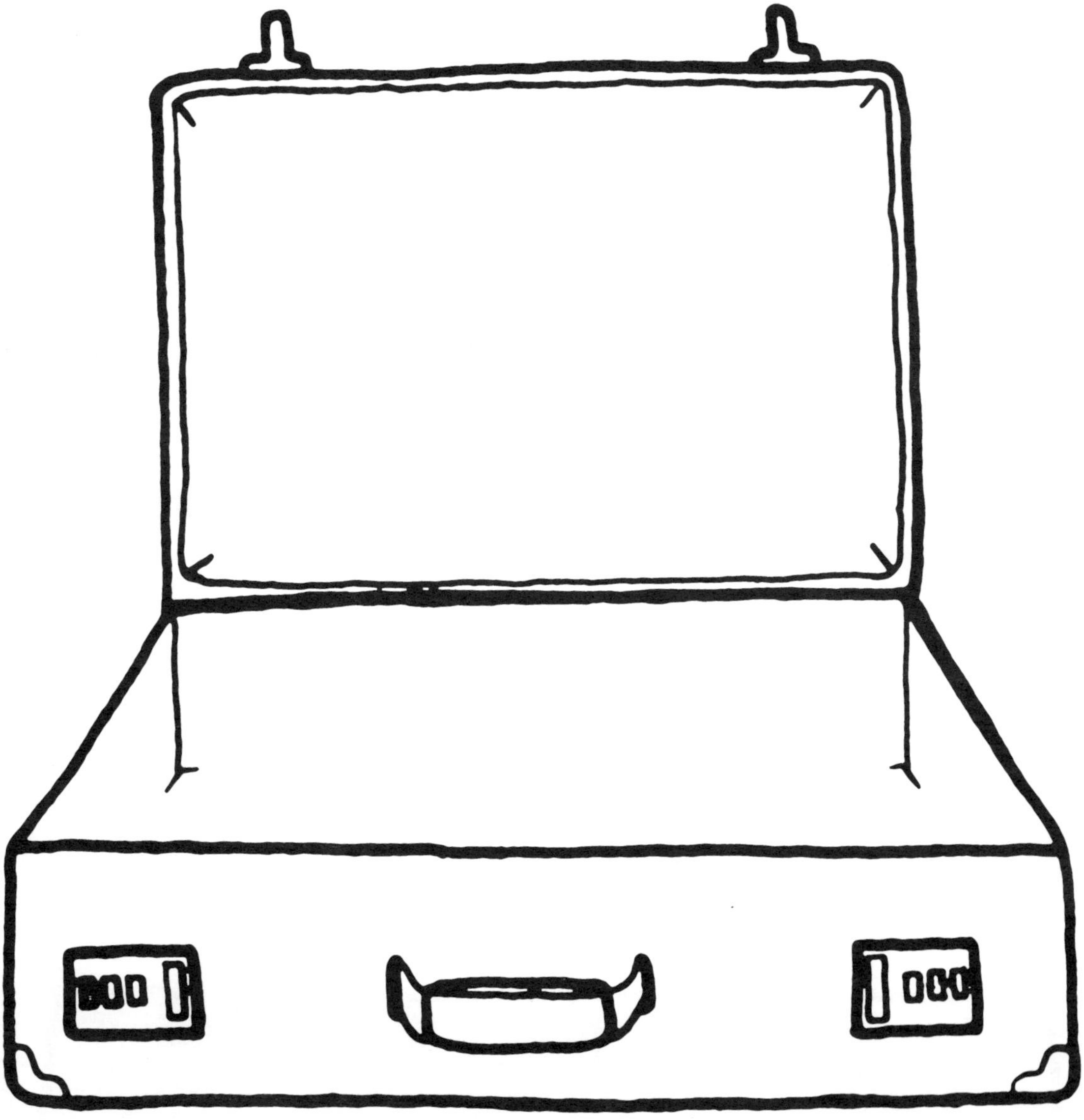

What's swinging in the park?

Draw your own cartoon character

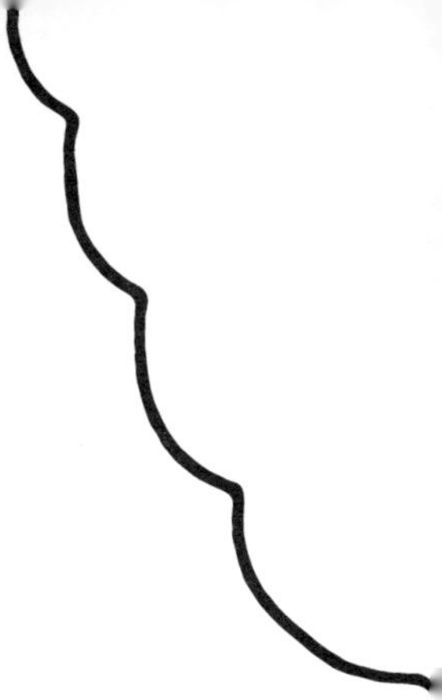

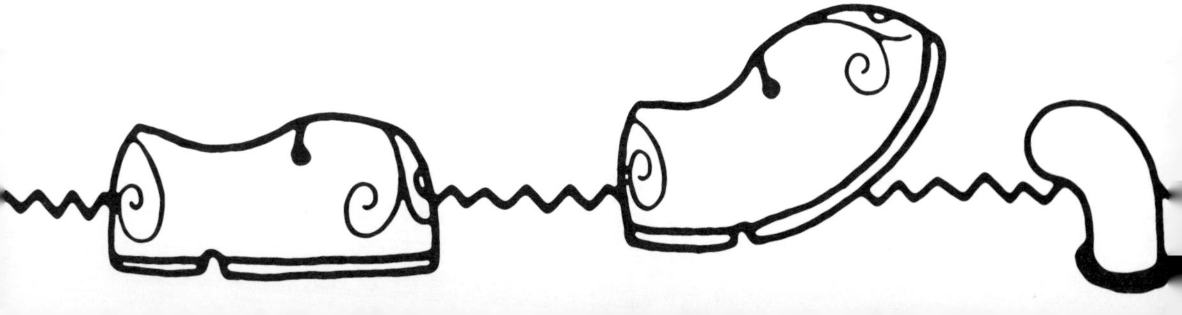

Sew the head back
on your favourite teddy

What are these?

Draw your own customized personal stereo

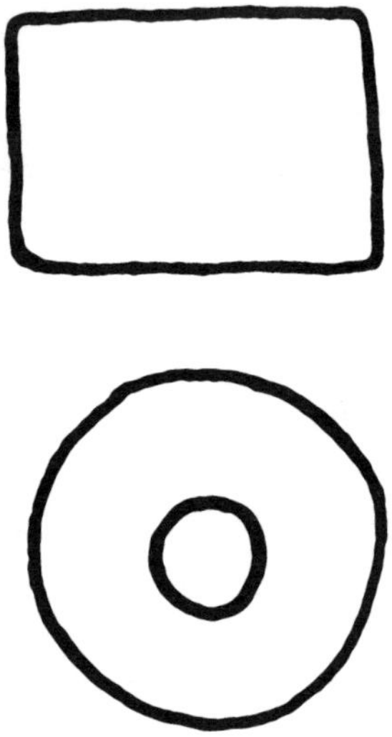

Join the dots?

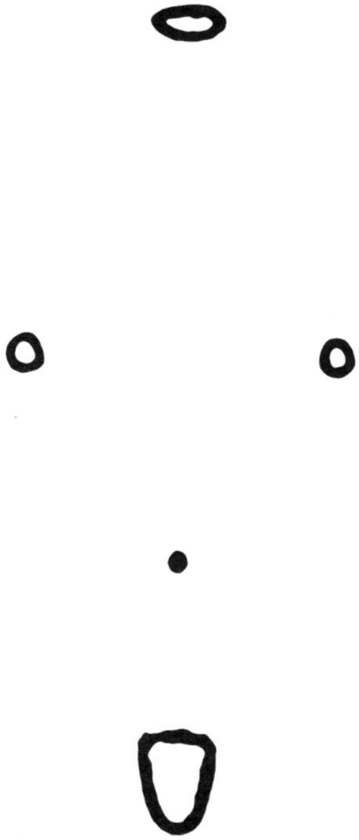

What's this?

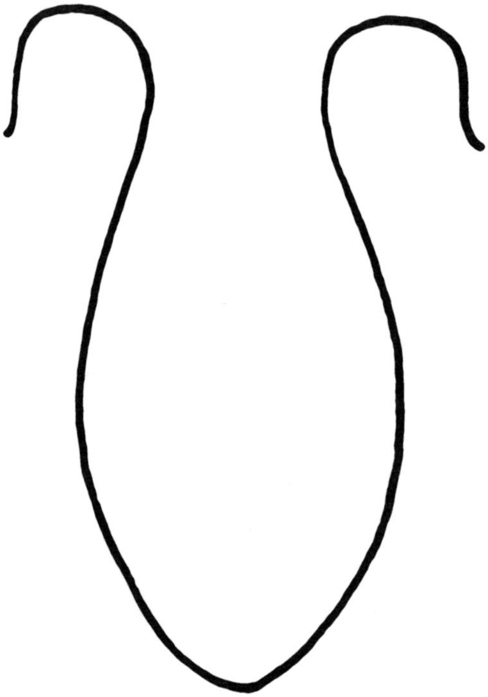

Is there something inside?

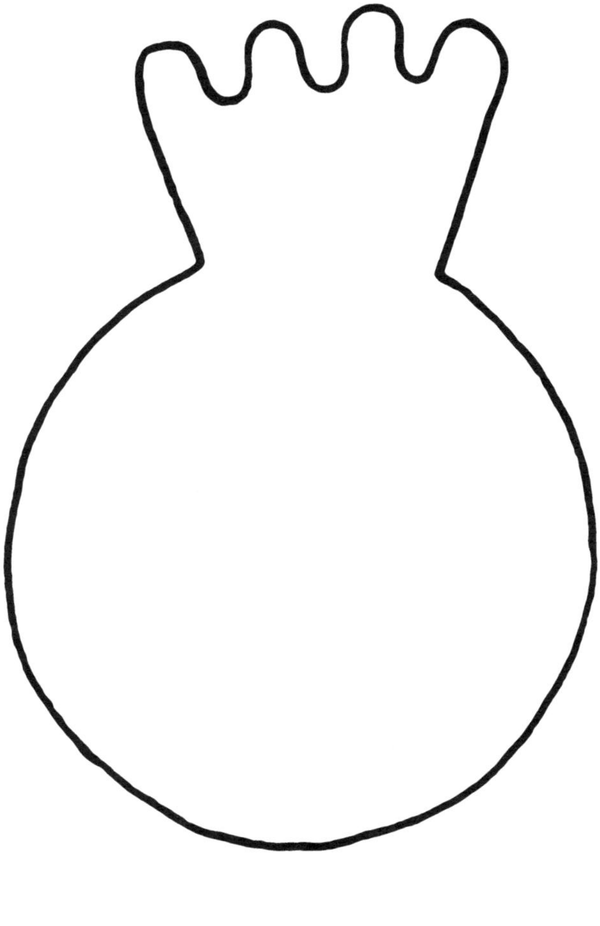

Draw a big balloon ride